URBAN SCHOOL
ADMINISTRATION

Edited by

TROY V. McKELVEY

and AUSTIN D. SWANSON

Department of Educational Administration
State University of New York at Buffalo

SAGE PUBLICATIONS, INC. / BEVERLY HILLS, CALIFORNIA

For information address:

SAGE PUBLICATIONS, INC.
275 South Beverly Drive
Beverly Hills, California 90212

First Printing

Printed in the United States of America

Standard Book Number: 8039-1008-8

Library of Congress Catalog Card No. 69-18750

Contents

Preface   9

[1] Integration or Apartheid?   15
TROY V. McKELVEY and AUSTIN D. SWANSON

Part I   21
THE EVOLUTION OF THE URBAN
COMMUNITY—Implications for the Schools

[2] Urban Growth and Educational Change   23
PAUL N. YLVISAKER

[3] Organizing Low-Income Neighborhoods
for Political Action   37
SAUL ALINSKY

Part II   49
RACIAL ISOLATION IN THE URBAN
COMMUNITY—Implications for the Schools

[4] School Segregation and Desegregation:
Some Misconceptions   51
DAVID K. COHEN

[5] School Community Relations in Large Cities   71
CHARLES E. STEWART

[6] Internal Action Programs for the Solution
of Urban Education Problems   93
MARIO D. FANTINI

Part III   107
SCHOOLS FOR THE URBAN
COMMUNITY—Need for Change

[7] Instructional Planning for the Urban Setting   109
SAMUEL SHEPARD, Jr.

[8] Recruitment and Retention of
Qualified Staff for City Schools   123
R. OLIVER GIBSON

[9] The Urban School System of Tomorrow   143
FRANK J. DRESSLER

Part IV   159
THE ORGANIZATION AND ADMINISTRATION
OF URBAN SCHOOLS

[10] Communication Problems in Large
Organizations   161
WARREN G. BENNIS

[11] The Governance of Education in
Metropolitan Areas   177
AUSTIN D. SWANSON

[12] Urban School Administration—Some
Problems and Futures   197
TROY V. McKELVEY

The Authors   215

URBAN SCHOOL
ADMINISTRATION

Preface

A GREAT CHALLENGE to education in urban centers today is the urgent need for equalizing educational opportunity through the racial and socioeconomic integration of school enrollments. To meet this challenge, more financial and human resources need to be directed toward increasing and improving knowledge and understanding of the school desegregation problem. Administrators and supervisors of school systems composing metropolitan areas, as well as university personnel who train the professional staffs of these schools, need to understand the effects of the desegregation problem on urban school administration.

For two weeks during the summer of 1967 seventy-five school administrators from the primary cities and the suburbs of the Buffalo, New York metropolitan area met together with faculty members of the State University of New York at Buffalo to study the challenges facing urban school administrators. The group invited several authorities in endeavors and disciplines related to the problem to share their insights with them. The chapters of this book, other than those authored by the editors, are the papers which these authorities presented.

The objectives of the Institute on Unique Problems of Urban School Administration were:

1. *To enhance the quality and the potential for creativeness of the educational leadership in the Buffalo metropolitan area through an extensive study of the nature of urban educational problems—particularly problems incident to school desegregation, social integration, and the equality of educational opportunity.*

2. *To provide two-way communication between the educational leaders in the Buffalo metropolitan area and the faculty of the State University of New York at Buffalo regarding the problems of the urban school in this region and the application of constructive recent thinking to the solution of urban educational problems.*

The chief financial support which permitted the idea of the Institute to be transformed into reality was provided by the United States Government under Title IV of the Civil Rights Act. The summer session of the State University of New York at Buffalo provided the meeting facilities and also contributed toward the honoraria of several of the special consultants. Financial support was also provided by Project Innovation, a regional supplementary education center funded under Title III of the Elementary and Secondary Education Act. Project Innovation funds supported those aspects of the Institute which directly involved urban and suburban superintendents of schools.

The Institute was planned around the perceived needs of the administrative staff of the Buffalo Public School System. The Buffalo Superintendent of Schools, Dr. Joseph Manch, and the Dean of the School of Education, State University of New York at Buffalo, Dr. Robert S. Fisk, appointed a representative

[10]

planning committee to discuss with, and to collect from, the Buffalo administrative staff their perceived needs regarding problem areas incident to school desegregation and the realization of equal educational opportunities. The survey data formed the basis for the selection of the special consultants whose papers are herein presented.

The Planning Committee, on the basis of the survey of needs, selected five major seminar topics to become the focus of the special seminars which met during the afternoon. Each seminar consisted of fifteen participants. Members of a seminar remained with the same group, exploring one topic for the entire two weeks. The following topics were the focus of seminar consideration under the indicated leadership:

1. School System Communication: Horizontal and Vertical,

2. School-Community Relations,

3. Recruitment and Retention of Qualified Staff for City Schools,

4. Instructional Planning,

5. Pre- and In-Service Education for Core Area Teachers.

The structure of the afternoon seminars was flexible, affording the participants opportunities to benefit from the contributions of several consultants during the Institute.

The participants of the Institute were selected from the administrative staffs of the Buffalo Public School System and selected large school systems which are a part of the greater Buffalo metropolitan area. Typical positions held by the participants were central office administrator or supervisor, principal, and assistant principal; also included were identified future administrative personnel who appeared on the school districts' administrative eligibility lists. Thus, the participants were local educational leaders who could collectively and individually contribute to the solution of urban educational problems.

It was evident from participant evaluation of the Institute that at least a portion of school administrators in the Buffalo metropolitan area are concerned enough about the problems their schools face to listen, to talk, and to take of their own time to do so. It also became clear that lack of horizontal communication was a major barrier to the development and implementation of new ideas within and among school districts of the area. The Institute provided a means for relaxed and free discussion among peers in a non-authoritarian setting. This could well have been the major benefit of the Institute. Means should be found for perpetuating this type of horizontal communication to supplement the traditional center-oriented communication system of large school systems. The participants also felt that a metropolitan university should offer such workshops, which are planned jointly with surrounding urban school districts, on a year-round basis.

A complete report of the Institute, its recommendations and its evaluation, is on file with the Special Training Program of the U.S. Office of Education.

The codirectors of the Institute (the editors of this volume) are indebted to many persons who contributed to its excellence. The major presenters were insightful and challenging, as the reader will soon discover. Harold Hefhe was editor of transcripts for those presentations which were extemporaneous. Appreciation is also expressed for the support given by Dr. Robert S. Fisk, Dean, School of Education, State University of New York at Buffalo; Dr. Joseph Manch, Superintendent of Schools,

Buffalo, New York; and Dr. Robert E. Lamitie, Director, Project Innovation. The codirectors acknowledge the significant contribution of the Seminar Leaders Warren Button, R. Oliver Gibson, Robert W. Heller and Chester Kiser, all Professors of Education at the State University of New York at Buffalo. Frank Ambrosie capably served as the Institute Coordinator. Finally, we wish to commend the participants for the wholesome attitude with which they approached their task. In the last analysis, it was the response of these people which permitted the Institute objectives to be realized and which stimulated the codirectors to share its contents with a larger audience through this volume.

Troy V. McKelvey
Austin D. Swanson

State University of New York
   at Buffalo
September 30, 1968

1

INTEGRATION OR APARTHEID?

TROY V. McKELVEY
and AUSTIN D. SWANSON

THE UNITED STATES is now an urban nation in spite of itself. We have not made the transition from an agrarian society gracefully; we still act and think as a rural nation. Our value structure remains oriented to rural conditions. Our political structure was designed for an agrarian economy and a sparse but relatively evenly distributed population. Some 70 per cent of the population now lives in urban areas, but we distrust these urban communities within which we live. Unhappily, the results are huge, sprawling, unplanned, ugly megalopolises which foster crime, violence, and civil disorders. These in turn have led a large portion of our youth, particularly the more thoughtful, to be disenchanted with society. All institutions are being challenged and the foundations of our society are being shaken. Changes will occur for good or for evil, depending upon our ability to cope with the realities of the time.

Perhaps we have never realized an open society, but if not, its closed nature was never so obvious as it is now. Today our people are fragmented according to economic, racial, and ethnic classifications. These groups live in different, relatively homogeneous, political subdivisions of the metropolitan area. They go to different schools, participate in and have available to them different recreational activities, and generally live in isolation from each other. If present policies persist, America is heading toward an apartheid society. The primary city of metropolitan areas and some of the older suburbs will be controlled by the poor and the black, surrounded by a white, middle class suburban ring. The differences between rich and poor and the differences between black and white, will then constitute an institutionalized polarization contrary to the goals of our constitutional democracy. We will have completed the evolution from an open to a closed society (Ylvisaker, Chapter 2).*

We are hampered in coping with the social changes which confront us because our social institutions are designed for the conditions of the rural nineteenth century. The dominant bureaucratic structure of organizations was designed for the stable, less technical, conditions of that century. The genius of mid-twentieth century America is change. To function effectively within this environment, organizations must have a structure which is adaptable, self-actuating, renewing, and which recognizes the highly specialized nature of today's workers (Bennis, Chapter 10; McKelvey, Chapter 12).

Urban educational institutions reflect the maladies of the metropolitan area as a whole, a fact which appears to be central to the solutions of their problems. School districts and school district boundaries grew out of the constraints of rural America. Metropolitan areas, even as late as thirty years ago, were essentially coterminus with the boundaries of the primary city; however, in the past thirty years virtually all metropolitan growth has been in the formerly rural political subdivisions contiguous to the primary city. Our inability to comprehend the scale of such growth, our mistrust of urban politics, and our whole mistrust of cities and urban areas in general have caused

---

*The citations in parentheses refer to subsequent chapters in this volume.

us to perpetuate these rural boundaries rather than to explore new ways of coping with size and to reorganize to reflect the organic metropolitan community (Swanson, Chapter II). Neighborhood schools are relics of the horse and buggy days, when it was necessary for a school to be within walking distance of every child's home. With the advances in transportation technology, this is no longer a requirement. Theoretically the schools have been freed to explore new types of organization, unfettered by the restraint of the distance a child can walk. However, loyalty to our rural traditions has prevented us from taking advantage of this technological development in urban areas, although the advances in rural areas have been quite significant (Cohen, Chapter 4). The bureaucratic organization is still the typical pattern for administering urban school districts. This is despite the fact that some districts—especially in the primary cities—have become so large that the organizations appear to be on the verge of collapse from their own weight.

The results of our tenacity to the old have been disastrous for public education. Our metropolitan schools are segregated, not only racially but also according to socioeconomic class. Our fragmentation of school districts and school attendance areas has resulted in great inequities and inequalities in educational opportunities. The resources available to school districts are not evenly distributed throughout the metropolitan area, nor are children who need special facilities and special programs. As a result, the children with the least educational disadvantage have been blessed with the most adequate facilities and programs, and those children with the greatest disadvantage have been denied adequate professional assistance in remedying their disadvantages. The net effect of all of this is that schools have ceased to function effectively in their role to prepare children for citizenship in a multi-ethnic, multisocial, democratic society

(Cohen, Chapter 4; Fantini, Chapter 6).

In this crisis, school people have assumed a posture of defensiveness. They have defended themselves against the attacks from the establishment; they have defended themselves against the attacks of reformers. They have not taken a position of leadership, remaining true to their traditional role as conservators. Here again is a traditional concept which needs re-evaluating. In the current state of crisis and confusion, those who know the problem best and those who know the processes best need to take positions of leadership. Educators must abandon their traditional conservative stance and assume a leadership role in building a new social order (Fantini, Chapter 6).

Recognizing the need for educational leadership, seventy-five administrators from schools in the Buffalo metropolitan area and faculty of the State University of New York at Buffalo met for two weeks to address themselves to these problems. They invited some of the nation's outstanding political and educational leaders and university scholars to meet with them. The transcripts of the papers presented by these authorities constitute the remainder of this volume. One general theme ran through all papers—change is here, and educators must adapt to it. The present urban crisis in the United States has been brought about by an obsession with self-interest and bigotry. The recent National Commission on Civil Disorders termed it "white racism." Countering this, the black people, who for three hundred years have been remarkably acceptant of their less-than-equal status, have begun to lose patience. This impatience has spawned the philosophy of Black Power, which in its extreme form is nothing more than black racism. If we continue on this path of white racism and black racism, the most pessimistic of the predictions included in the following

[18]

chapters will become a reality. If the American people, however, will take a hard, critical look at themselves and act according to the principles to which they give lip service, the dreams of the most optimistic will be but a beginning to the achievements which we as a united nation can realize.

The solution to the crisis as it relates to education requires a three-step sequence: providing access for all segments of the community to the decision-making process, the development of workable programs which combine the concepts of compensatory and quality-integrated education, and the reorganization of education in urban areas.

First, the voiceless segments of metropolitan communities must find a voice. All citizens must be involved in making the decisions which will shape the restructuring of the schools. In suburban areas the citizens already have this ability. As a matter of fact, their concern over maintaining a strong voice in educational policies is one of their major objections to metropolitan approaches to educational problems. The bureaucratic structure of the primary city schools, however, has left both rich and poor, black and white, without significant voice in the determination of educational policy. This can be overcome in part by assuming new organizational structures which would give more independence to schools from central office regulation. It also requires, especially in poor and black neighborhoods, people organizing in a fashion that permits them to fully participate in the political dialogue of the community (Alinsky, Chapter 3; Fantini, Chapter 6).

There appears to be no argument as to the ultimate necessity of an integrated school structure. Dr. Samuel Shepard said during the Institute, "We live in a multiracial, multi-ethnic society. If the goal of education is to prepare children for

[19]

effective citizenship in a democratic society, we cannot justify educating them in isolation because it is contrary to the accomplishment of that goal" (Shepard, Chapter 7). The evidence that all children prosper in an integrated setting is overwhelming (Cohen, Chapter 4). However, the reality of the situation is that integration will be a long time coming to many metropolises. How do you integrate Harlem? How do you integrate Washington, D.C.? How do you integrate Detroit? How do you integrate St. Louis? It may be possible, but it will take at least a generation.

Thus, the second step in meeting the urban education crisis is to develop workable programs of compensatory education while working toward the ultimate goal of quality integrated education. Small class size, the most modern equipment, and revised curricula will not produce better results among disadvantaged children unless the attitude of the teacher is one which expects results. Success also depends upon support of the home, and support of the home will not be forthcoming unless teachers and administrators genuinely welcome and seek parental cooperation (Shepard, Chapter 7; Stewart, Chapter 5).

Structure also matters. The present educational structure is dysfunctional for the purpose of providing all children with a quality integrated education. The third step in meeting the urban education crisis is to reorganize public education in the metropolitan areas so that this objective may be realized. This will require totally new thinking about community, class, neighborhood, school, and responsibility. It will involve new structures for governing public education and new structures for administering learning (Dressler, Chapter 9; McKelvey, Chapter 12). But none of this will happen without a major change of attitudes in the American people—white, black, rich, middle class and poor.

[20]

Part I

THE EVOLUTION

OF THE

URBAN COMMUNITY

IMPLICATIONS FOR

THE SCHOOLS

2

URBAN GROWTH AND EDUCATIONAL CHANGE

PAUL N. YLVISAKER

EVERY INSTITUTION in the United States is now under threat. Every guild, every profession is undergoing crisis. This includes everything from the Boy Scouts to the church, from the lawyers to the doctors to the labor leaders, government personnel, and educators. A vast number of signals are coming in at us that we still cannot quite interpret. There is a tremendous temptation underneath this shower of signals to begin relapsing into routine types of responses using the conventional wisdom of the guild. The responses are resulting in a form of retreatism.

Our society is entering a period that requires a resurgence of what you might call law and order and security. But it requires simultaneously, a relinquishing of much of what has been authoritarian which our younger generation is rebelling against. There is some propriety in this revolution and there are some improprieties. There are some reckless qualities and there are some very courageous qualities. Above all there are energetic qualities which I think this country must use.

The Breaking up of Traditional Society

The activity within society today can be compared to the activity within an atomic pile. What we have done literally is to crack the social atom. These social atoms are small scale organizations with fixed membership, in which an individual knows his place — such as in the village or extended family. One can go to the villages outside Mexico City and still see where generations have lived through hundreds of years with no change in status or position. A kind of stasis exists in these villages that the Japanese perfected in their medieval era and which the Greeks tried to perfect thousands of years ago. One can see the breaking up of these social atoms as the highway comes out to the villages from Mexico City. The same thing happened when the cheap airline fare went to Puerto Rico. A similar reaction occurred when our railroads, buslines, and then our super highways, dipped into the migrant pools of Negroes, Puerto Ricans, Mexican-Americans, and Appalachians within the United States. You can see what happens when a rural family is touched by that line of intrusion; the atom gets split. When the individual from that static society moves into Mexico City, New York City, Akron, Buffalo, or Chicago, he moves into what we call the urban setting. He moves into the atomic pile where the high energy forces begin to break up the fixed patterns in which he has lived. Urbanization and industrialization are really nothing more than individualization. The individual is pulled from his fixed atom. This process is accompanied by the release of a tremendous amount of energy.

Unfortunately, I would argue that what we have done in our cities, our atomic piles, is to forget to put in the lead rods. As a matter of fact, we don't know what the social equivalents to the lead rods are, nor do we know how to adjust them. As a result, we're getting atomic piles that are going out of control. A tremendous amount of social energy is being dissipated into the heat of social conflict. It is this loss of human power that is the social failure of our twentieth century. That power must be expressed positively. It has been liberated, but if we don't control it with some device like lead rods in the atomic pile we'd better watch out because this uncontrolled, undirected energy can destroy. This is the situation in the ghetto in the United States today—fantastic energies, bottled-up, and exploding. The challenge for all of us, especially those of us in education, is to recognize that a chain reaction is taking place; to give it shape, to give it direction, and to harness this fantastic power which has been released by urbanization and individual-ization.

My generation, and the one before me, and the one after me, are milling up behind a dam of understanding. There's another society just beyond where we are. I'm not sure what that society is, but we can hear sounds over the dam, the splashing of new currents. We're beginning to sense its dimensions, beginning to grope for a feeling of its nature.

The most impressive portion of General Marshall's 1947 speech at Harvard, where he gave expression to the Marshall Plan, occurred in the middle of that talk when the General stopped, took off his glasses, looked at the audience, and in the only unprepared part of that address, said, "You know, our problems these days are so incredibly complex that a man of any integrity must bow down to God when he tries to deal with them." There was a hush. He put his glasses on and went back to his text. But it was that pause that gave me the clue to the Marshall era. It is that pause that I sense when I talk to any head of any institution now groping. The kids coming after us

[25]

sense it. They sense it in many ways. They listen for the phonics. They're not going to fall for the illusion that somebody is the Wizard of Oz with the power or wisdom to correct and solve all of our problems.

You see it in the local setting when a Mexican-American family comes across the border into East Los Angeles, the father literally broken in his life, not knowing the answer to the city. The village truths don't seem to apply. New truths or half-truths seem to be the rule of the day. The only structure for the younger generation in that family seems to be the peer group which acts with the reckless confidence of youth. These kids begin on the family, the teacher, the police, the mayor, the governor, the president, the heads of institutions. They begin groping, as they've been taught to do in this Dr. Spock generation. This is a questioning generation, precocious in its perceptions. It has learned through every pore and by every sense, in front of television, which has been used as a baby sitting device since age two, three, and four. It has learned about uncertainty by watching Churchill, de Gaulle, and Kennedy, struggling with problems beyond even their capacities. This generation is now beginning to smack up behind us, against this wall of uncertainty.

I have a feeling that education should give expression to this uncertainty, make it creative, and invite these kids to search for answers. We need that energy to help us break through the dam that's keeping us from a comprehension of the next society we're going to deal with. It's been interesting and challenging to me to use my job in New Jersey as I used my job with the Ford Foundation, to teach. Somehow I have the feeling there is not enough in the repository of human knowledge on current problems to go through the process of conventional education

[26]

with its routine, its imagery and its symbolism, term after term. The job is not to communicate what we now know, but *to add* by the creative search and to extend the invitation to this generation to join the search. I have noticed the response of this generation. The energy of these young kids working with me on the job reaps tremendous returns in the face of towering responsibilities. I think that the apprenticeship may be coming back into vogue as an educational device when attached (and I'm not going to plead that I am one) to some of the master teachers out there on the job.

If a bomb dropped on Princeton destroying its immediate environs, you could find equally as good a faculty in the adjacent perimeter. If you in turn bombed that area, you could go out in the next mile of the radius, and in that outer sector find equally as good a faculty. You find these teachers in surprising places; the obvious ones are the electronic laboratories. You find them also at a very grubby level in very unexpected places. You find people who have had to survive twenty to thirty years of living with things not completely comprehended or completely taught. But they have had the capacity to learn and therefore gladly teach. We've missed something because we've been teaching more and more from the top of society. We've missed realizing that those lower on the totem pole can also teach.

Let me go back again to another realm of the setting that we deal with. I'd like to stretch your minds. I'd like to take you up on a mountain of historical perspective, to look as Toynbee would look at the unfolding of America and the world during the next thirty year period. Brace yourself because it's not going to be an optimistic presentation.

[27]

The Next Thirty Years

We are now three billion people with an average income of $477.00. That means that a person of average income is considerably poorer than one would find in the American ghetto today. In the next thirty years there will be another three billion people in the world with an average income projected at $500.00 per capita. This may give you an idea of the kind of world we are going to be walking into. A world highly competitive for its resources, moving incredibly fast. There will be television sets in every community. You will not be able to hide the facts of life from any group. All will know immediately what the circumstances of their kinfolk is in every community around the world. These numbers will be living mostly in the crowded metropolitan areas. You will be lucky to be born in something like Hong Kong. You will, on the average, perhaps be born into the circumstances of Calcutta, with literally hundreds of thousands of people sleeping on the streets. The world that faces us is a world of incipient and present poverty and we are an island of affluence in that world. Americans are going to come hard to this feeling of being the French aristocrats of the twentieth century, tied together with the industrial nations of Europe, part of Latin America, some emerging countries, and the Soviet Union. This may sound like a strange coalition, but these nations must themselves make alliances with us to survive as part of the island of affluence in this world of thirty years hence. Situations similar to what is happening in Vietnam will probably light up in other places throughout these thirty years hence. People in poverty will resent the fact that they are outside the industrial system and will want to take their share of it.

The situation inside the island of affluence is precisely the same, though in differing proportions. We now have one-sixth of our population, half of what it was thirty years ago, in the same circumstances of feeling on the outside. They will be joined by a fair percentage of others, who will resent their poverty with increased restlessness as they are pulled out of the bondage of the farm, the small family, the small community by this urban release. What we have seen this summer, I am afraid, is merely a point along a rising curve, unless we do something sizable and dramatic about it.

Being the affluent minority, we will be forced into two types of responsibilities: (1) a militaristic response to defend what we have; (2) a humanistic response in which we use every measure at our disposal to assist and improve the conditions of the have-nots. The temptation to use the militaristic approach is very great.

The Defensive or Humanistic Response

I was on riot duty in New Jersey. I saw what happens in the escalation of security response. The beginning incident, rightly or wrongly, explodes the tinder and the tinder spreads past the capacity of the local police to control it. The state police are called in, then the national guard, and in the case of Detroit, the federal troops. Escalation by one group produces a similar response by the other group. We were lucky in New Jersey to be able to de-escalate fairly quickly. I will not debate at this point whether we were slow or fast in turning the curve.

A very important thing happened to us during the height of the crisis. Two young men who had gone to complete their education in the ghetto on their own, came to us at night and told us what escalation past this point would do. The rioters were creating an army against us. Each act on our part compounded the numbers of those ready to respond against us. The guerrillas and the snipers began increasing. The resentments built up. There was danger that what had started with a fraction of one per cent would spread through the Negro community and then the white community until major fractions of both populations would be at war with each other. To counter this we de-escalated. Normalcy returned, but barely.

The temptation to escalate defensive maneuvers against the threat of disorder is going to characterize our society throughout the next decade. To be able concurrently to remain constructive and humanitarian will strain every fiber of the American tradition of civil liberties. The magnitude of the problem may be better understood if it is put into some statistical terms. The ghetto in the United States is now growing by 500,000 Negroes per year. Merely to keep the ghetto its present size will require the movement of a half-million Negroes into white areas. The present rate is 50,000. If this does not happen, over the next five years a city a year will become predominantly Negro. The rate picks up so that by 1983, twenty to twenty-five of our major central cities will be predominantly Negro. This may be good in one sense, because it would give the American Negro political power for the first time in his own constituency.

But the future for the predominantly Negro urban center is not bright. The politics of transition are not pleasant politics. We can recall historically what happened when the Irish took over Boston and turned it into a kind of Sherwood Forest with Robin Hood and his merry men fleecing every tax payer from the Boston community who wandered through. It took a long time to change. It made for pleasant legendry and very bad civics.

[30]

What the Negro is going to inherit in the central city is the deficit area of the American economy. Forty per cent of those Negroes will be in poverty. Employment possibilities are dwindling and housing conditions are worsening in the ghetto.

We now stand where President Lincoln stood in 1860. He had to risk the Union to save it. President Johnson now faces precisely this in historical perspective. We face the prospect of a United States divided politically, not North and South, but central cities vs. suburban communities. Will we be able to react to this positively or are we going to continue to duck it and deal by the rule of incrementalism? All 440 federal grant programs put together, many of which I've helped engineer and defend, are not doing much to change or alter these trends. The magnitudes are of an order beyond present scale. This summer has shown that we face a national problem. Eighty to ninety communities exploding simultaneously in protest. And given proportions of the problem, even with the most benign and dramatic kind of measures that we can now produce, the situation will get worse before it gets better.

As I look through the pattern of these riots, I get some confusing signals. I saw it as a race war in the ghetto of Plainfield and Newark. Then I saw it as a youthful rebellion and then as a kind of civil breakdown. Then in Detroit, new signals came in: whites and Negroes were looting in concert. Elsewhere, it was a rumble—not so much between white and black, but between the toughs of both colors. When I saw the disconnected youths within the ghetto, and the disconnected outside the ghetto, I began to wonder whether we were dealing with something more basic than race and disadvantage. There appears to be some evidence of disconnectedness within elements of the Dr. Spock generation which includes elements

[31]

of the Vietnam GI returnee. A disconnectedness that goes deep—so deep that people are "cutting out" from this society. The atomic pile melting, releasing destructive energies.

I also saw something in the middle of the riots that gave me encouragement. It became my lot to go in there twenty-four hours after the first policeman had been brutally beaten to death and to face hundreds of angry residents of that Negro community. Frankly, I never thought I was going to get out alive, but the very act of going down there without police protection somehow seemed to show some of the disconnected, who were relatively few, that something was different here. Some of them came back to city hall that night, and we began a negotiation that strained the credibility of many in that city—but a process in which those from the ghetto began to feel listened to and responsible.

I noticed in that setting that the same people, the "disconnected," who were ready to go the route of violence were also ready to work constructively. Now our problem is to harness our ambivalent responses: simultaneously to constrain the tendency toward violence, and to give opportunity to those psychologically outside the system to participate responsibly in it. We can minimize neither the need for law and order nor the need to make certain that the lowest man on the social totem pole feels it is also *his* and *his* order.

What's going to be the response? How can we strike a balance between the defensive and humanistic approach? Are we going to retreat to the suburbs? A recent issue of a national magazine has a long article on the nice places in America left to live. They list all of America that's pleasant and free of racial problems. You can just see the run on those communities. No

[32]

doubt many of us are ready to flee further, and to retreat in other ways as well—leaving the job to the paid bureaucrat, the poverty program, the welfare worker, the teacher—hoping that by some magic the whole bothersome problem will wash away.

A Long-Range Social Strategy

But if we can curb our escapism, we can handle the problem. The necessary ingredients start with national leadership: to tell America what the problem is and to describe its dimensions. To look beyond the improvised approach which says we'll do this and this and this and three gimmicks will get you through the summer. We need a ten to twenty year social strategy. Unless the strategy is there, unless the statement of the problem in these dimensions is there, I fear we're going to panic and waste energy and time on short-run immediate responses. We'll be pushed toward escalating security forces, toward doubling the expenditures in programs that don't necessarily cut the mustard, and into throwing away the poverty program for some reasons that may or may not really be valid.

Certainly to survive this decade, we'll have to go at least to the scale equivalent with our effort in Vietnam, not necessarily in expenditure but in commitment. Newark, Detroit, Jersey City, and all other ghettoed and declining cities of this country should be rebuilt in the next ten to fifteen years on a production schedule, using the resources of the great construction and finance companies. They must be rebuilt by critical path methods which incorporate the demands of adequate relocation. Whatever we do must be done tangibly and by deadline so we do not have the urban renewal promises that lag and end up with benefit to only one sector of the

[33]

community. It's going to have to be a participatory kind of operation. We've got to get the disconnected back into feeling they've got a stake in this. We've got to have the cooperation of the 90 per cent who want to be middle class so that their sympathies are with the constructive effort rather than with the destructive effort.

The educator's job is a fantastic one. He's got to come out of his isolation. He can no longer talk in the abstract about non-partisan politics, which in practice has led to partisan education. He has to get into the mix and never make a decision until a cross-section of the community has somehow been contended with; its interests faced; and its people talked to. The process of making a decision is often more important than the decision itself. The school system is also going to have to let itself outside of its walls and its campuses to where the action is. Education more and more is in life, a search for something other than the conventional. Teaching is going on out there. The kids know it and they're going where the teaching is even if it's through their own experience. We're also going to have to deal with some lost sheep. The symbolism of Christ leaving the ninety-nine to go for one is very crucial at this point. We have the disconnected one out of a hundred in American society—white, young, Negro, poor, affluent. He's sometimes unreachable because of high ability, sometimes unreachable because of low ability. Now is the time when the efforts of education and the educator are going to have to go to that one lost sheep.

We are also going to have to carry some other social burdens. We've recruited our police in this country largely from the immigrant group who made it just before the Negro emigrated to the city. We have expected peace at a line of confrontation where there is competition and a built-in hostility. It's easy for us in the suburbs to talk about it, but it is rough to live with if you are a part of either competing group.

The church and parochial education have a special responsibility at this stage. Their schools, often in the central cities, can become another form of white escapism. Their small groups and their benevolent societies can easily become places of hate. I speak this candidly because I know the young church. Episcopalian, Lutheran, Jewish, Catholic, the movement in the young church (which includes some older Turks as well) is a very encouraging one. This kind of movement on the other side of the line must accompany the movement in the ghetto to reduce tensions and pressures.

I've watched political leaders—from the White House, to the governor, to the mayor. They are lonely men in lonely places making decisions where civilization hangs on a slender line. The temptation is to unleash force, to curtail humanitarianism. There are going to be many rough moments these coming years—more than a few political casualties—a lot of almost impossible jobs left by a society that has consistently swept its problems under the rug. The constructive side of America is really being challenged. I just hope it will respond.

3

ORGANIZING LOW-INCOME NEIGHBORHOODS FOR POLITICAL ACTION

SAUL ALINSKY

THE INDUSTRIAL AREAS Foundation of Chicago, which I represent, is involved in the development of mass organization in low income areas such as the Negro ghetto and low income white communities. During the 1950s we worked with the Mexican-Americans on the West Coast and throughout the Southwest. The Back of the Yards Council, which was our first major project about twenty years ago, involved organizing the people in the slums back of the stockyards in Chicago. This area was the nadir of all slums in America. It was worse than Harlem; it was unbelievable. It was the site of Upton Sinclair's *The Jungle*.

The philosophy behind the mass organization of the have-nots involves two premises which are directly involved in life or education. It is difficult for me to draw a dichotomy between life and education. It concerns itself with an understanding of what these large sectors of democratic DP's—dropouts or kickouts of the democratic society—mean for America; the relationship of the poor to us today and to our future. A discussion of education is a discussion of people. Specifically, it involves a revolutionary changing society which can no longer be coped with in the static, segmented philosophy typified by the school buildings currently in use. The same negative outlook is characteristic of the kinds of teaching approaches of the past two or three generations. Massive changes, such as the mobility of the population, the relativity of values, or the use of mass media, cannot be neglected.

The problems faced by our revolutionary fathers have a bearing on the issues concerned with the organization of people in low income areas. Madison, Hamilton, Monroe, Adams, and Franklin had their disagreements but they were extraordinary politically sophisticated men. It would be very difficult to find another band of revolutionaries better read and more versed in political philosophy and basic fundamental questions of life; in short, more politically literate. Jefferson's correspondence, now being published by the Princeton University Press, reveals the torture he experienced as he attempted to determine whether people, or how many people, in fact, are basically desirous of being free men. He felt that some people had not developed to the point where they could accept the price of freedom—the price being not only the ability to make decisions, but also to bear the personal responsibility for the effect of those decisions. This is a problem of very great concern in communities today. People are fearful of accepting responsibility for their decisions. This unwillingness to accept responsibility is especially evident in those communities that approach me to come in and organize. When I tell them that we are short of staff and would prefer to train some of their people to do the job, at a much lower cost to them, the response is always the same, "No thank you, you take the responsibility." If something such as a riot occurs, churches and other groups want to be in a position to turn and say, "If we'd known Alinsky was going to go that far, we never would have had anything to do with him. But we didn't know. It's his fault." This is the basic gesture of mankind, the Pilate hand-washing ritual.

Responsibility–The Price of Freedom

The assumption of responsibility, the price of freedom, is a major problem in organizing people in low income areas. It is just as much a problem in any other sector of middle or upper class society. The revolutionary fathers were not the kind of idealists who made the mistake common to most people and particularly so in the field of education, that of mixing up two worlds; the world as it is and the world as we would like it to be. In the world as it is, the right things are done almost invariably for the wrong reason. In the world as it is, man acts out of self-interest rather than out of a mystical altruism. In this world, morality is more or less a rationalization of one's position on the power pattern at a particular time. If you're a have-not, you're out to get, and you develop a morality that justifies this. It is then that you appeal to a law higher than man-made law; you've got to, because the establishment made the laws. On the other hand, if you're part of the establishment and your drive is to keep, you subscribe to the morality of responsibility, of law and order, and education. You don't want change.

[39]

The point I am trying to make is that the whites in America will suddenly have the divine revelation that segregation, after all, is "Un-Christian," "Un-American," and "Gives aid and comfort to the Communists" when they have moved so far out into the suburbs that it takes them half a day to get to work and a half-day to get back. Then, and on that basis, they will reject segregation, and rationalize and justify a course of action according to the reason just mentioned.

The American revolutionary leaders knew the difference between the world as it is and the world as they would like it to be. They knew very well that many of the principles they were enunciating were those to be achieved in the world ahead of us. They had violent disagreements on many points. You may recall from the Federalist papers how they disagreed over the issue of whether or not the poor and uneducated should have equal political power, the right to vote. There was great concern on the part of Hamilton as to whether or not people who were illiterate or poor should be trusted with a ballot. However, Hamilton was a political realist and knew that in the world as it is one never has a choice of what is best. Choice in all of life is always made in terms of the alternatives which are available. As a democratic realist Hamilton knew he had to agree with Madison and Jay that the votes should be distributed across the board regardless of property and education because to do otherwise would mean the end of the democratic way and the beginning of a life of aristocracy. And so he conceded. But through it all, there was the recognition that in this society you have to keep striving for change in order to ultimately achieve the kind of life which provides equal opportunity for all. These men understood the changing character of life. They knew that as long as people have the opportunity and ability to act they will be able to meet and resolve their problems. They will have

[40]

it within them to do it. This is the democratic way.

Equal Opportunity for Political Action

The one thing that would kill the democratic dream would be if a substantial sector of our people were deprived of an opportunity for political action. This is the reason why any student of the future of a free society has to be concerned with its internal character. The problems that currently exist within our society need immediate attention because they threaten our way of life. It is a contradiction to be a segregationist and at the same time be committed to a free society for yourself. However, life itself is a continuum of contradictions. To be committed to a free society and to the future of a free society, one must of necessity, on a purely political basis, stand completely for integration. This is one of the major ideas behind the organization of B.U.I.L.D. (Build Unity, Independence, Liberty, and Dignity) in Buffalo. Power, and I quote from Webster's unabridged dictionary, is "the ability to act." B.U.I.L.D. is organized to create the opportunity to act.

Organization—The Key to Representation

There is another basic reason for organization. Unless a community is organized, there is no way to get representation from that community. Imagine the situation. Suppose our establishment were to wake up some morning and have a revelation. As a result they would say, "You know, everything we've been doing has been wrong. We've been looking down on these ghettos as though we were the big ruling power. We've been doing things for them. We've been sending in colonial representatives in the guise of various kinds of professional people. We've been giving them a little teaching, a little clinic, a little this, a little that. Our churches have sent in missionaries. We put in some settlement houses. Our whole outlook has been what we might call a 'zoo-keeper' mentality. We do these things to keep the animals quiet. We haven't permitted them to choose their representatives. We've always picked those people that we considered to be fit to represent them—people who agree with us." (Up until the last six or seven years, when the mayor of a city decided to appoint someone to represent the Negro community on his commissions, or whatever he created, he always picked a school principal or a minister.)

Suppose our establishment went on to say, "One of the big problems in the Negro ghetto is that the people have never really been able to chose their own representatives. But from now on we're going to stop this whole approach of colonialism. We're going to stop working *for* people, which means that we regard them as inferior. We're going to accept them and work *with* them. We want to meet with their representatives to work out a joint program." Then the establishment would turn to the ghetto and say, "Send us your representatives." Who would they send? If this were to happen under ordinary circumstances, who would represent the Negro community? It becomes impossible to have representatives unless a community is organized. There is a revolutionary difference between making decisions for a community and having a community's own representatives sit down with other sectors of society and start the give and take and the discussion and the bargaining of the democratic process.

This is why B.U.I.L.D. is so important to the Negro community in Buffalo. They will be able to turn to the city and

[42]

say, "We from this community represent so many people and so many organizations. We are here to talk with you." It is here that you have the necessary physical links to start the communication and the democratic bargaining. Without that it becomes literally impossible. You cannot have the democratic process and you cannot have the democratic involvement of people in the community as long as they are not organized—as long as they do not have representation. If they are not organized they don't have the circumstances from which they can derive legitimate representation. This is the fundamental requirement for the democratic mix.

Education—The Development of Curiosity

It is at this point that we begin to see the importance of education. As people start getting organized—as they start getting power—for the first time there is a reason for education. There is a real incentive for them to begin questioning. What this means, very simply, is that education is really the development of a passionate curiosity, a questioning of things about you. It causes you to ask the whys. Why is this? Why is that? When an organization turns to city hall and asks, "What do you mean doing this? Why are you doing it?" it has begun to learn. This is one of the fundamental changes that occur in a community at the time it is being organized.

This idea of the importance of being organized in order to have true representation from the community holds true for the schools as well. Principals or administrators who have ideas about community involvement in the operation of the school must, of necessity, have a method of securing legitimate representation from the community.

[43]

One of the biggest hangups we have in the democratic process is that educators who are committed to democracy, just like most other people, may accept intellectually and verbally the democratic ideals in terms of equality, but not accept them emotionally. This goes for a lot of white teachers in Negro schools. We have our hangups inside where it becomes very schizy. We say one thing in terms of our political tradition, but react emotionally to the contrary.

One of the first jobs we have to do in organization is to convince the leaders in the local ghetto communities to have faith in their own people. When they first come together they start their attack on the outside society by saying, "You know what they call our people? They call them stupid slobs. This is what the outside communities really think of our people." At the same time we detect within those local community leaders a lack of faith in their own people. They feel this way because while they are busy meeting, talking about organizations, considering what has to be done to bring about change, the rest of the people are just sitting around, uninterested. Building confidence between people in the low income community is a basic goal in our organizational strategy.

There is also a feeling of personal incompetency which affects the masses of people in the low income community. When you ask them what's wrong with the schools, they say: "Anybody can see what's wrong with them. The teachers are no good. They send in crummy teachers, substitute teachers." When we ask them what they would do about it they say, "You change it. Get rid of segregation for one thing. You guys are responsible for this mess to begin with so it's your problem. You figure it out. You change it."

[44]

There is a reason for this kind of attitude. When people feel that there is nothing they can do about a problem, that they do not have the power to make any changes, they don't think about it. This goes for any kind of people, in any part of society, and for any kind of problem. As long as you feel that there's nothing you can do about it, why beat your brains out? Why think about it? But as soon as you get the kind of situation where power begins to come into the hands of the people, where for the first time they feel they have an opportunity, a real opportunity to make changes, they begin to ask questions about the schools which are meaningful. What is a good teacher? What is a bad teacher? How do you get good teachers? How do you get rid of bad teachers? Not until these people are in a situation where they feel they can do something about an institution or about a problem is there reason for them to wake up—to get turned on. As they ask these questions, they themselves are well down the road to education. Basically, this is what education is. The person who leaves college with the curiosity to ask questions has been educated. God help the person who's spent four years memorizing notes from lectures that will enable him to pass the examinations at the end of the term. In a sense, he's spent four years being a portable garbage can.

The process of organization is an educational process. A few weeks ago I spent some time on the Indian reserves in Canada in response to their request to have me assist them organize. They want change. They want to put a stop to the injustices they have been suffering, but they want to retain their own value structure. They argued that the formation of pressure groups to seek repeal of the Indian Act would mean exposure to and involvement in the corruption of white man's society. Their appeal to me was, "Show us another way."

There isn't any other way. You either get with it or you're out of it. This is the way it's been since the time mankind began. You organize to get power—the ability to act—or you don't get it.

As I questioned them, they gave their reasons against organizing on a militant basis—their wonderful set of values. This rationale has been used for years and it's been accepted by the intellectuals in the universities who have a real romantic hangup when it comes to problems of the poor and problems of minority groups. The problem is that both of these groups want to believe this thing. The Indians want to believe their rationale in order to justify their inaction, and some of the intellectuals want to believe it because they have a romantic projection on one side and on the other side they are upset with the seeming bankruptcy of our own materialistic values. To them the Indian values represent something like Shangri-la.

"Look," I said, "if you don't want to organize and go out and fight for your rights, then you're saying that you're satisfied in just living on your welfare checks." To that, some of the Indian leaders replied, "See, that's where you don't understand. You whites are degraded by accepting welfare but it's different with us. You whites owe it to us. We are not degraded by taking welfare because you took our land away, therefore, you owe it to us. We're just getting a small payment back from you. We still have our dignity." (This is an interesting rationale.) I responded by pointing out that practically every people at one time or another had had their land taken away, but they did not resign themselves to perpetual mourning. Then they go on to say, "We want a creative life which you don't have because your values are so destructive." And I say, "Give me an example of what you mean by a creative life." They say,

"Well, if a man wants to spend his life fishing, that's being creative. The government should support him."

It went on and on from one absurdity to another on the basis of one straight question after another until finally they turned the corner. They came around the other way. But they were badly shook about it. One of the Canadian educators remarked afterward, "For the first time it occurred to me that the Greeks really knew what they were doing when they killed Socrates. He was stirring up a revolution just by asking questions."

Basically, that's what the whole education process is. Through education, whether it be in our public schools, our private schools, or in our colleges, we should attempt to get people to ask questions because people who ask questions are restless. They're not willing to sit around, be turned off, and uninvolved. A future of a people as free people depends upon their asking questions. That is why asking questions is the most dangerous, the most subversive thing you can do in a totalitarian state. It cannot be tolerated.

The primary goal of education in a free society should be the development of an inquiring mind. People have got to be encouraged to ask questions. It's why? Why? Why? These whys are the cutting edge of life itself. Why should I take this? Just because you're white and I'm black, why does that make you any better?

What I hope and what I know will be happening in Buffalo is that through action—it's through action that we really learn—these kinds of questions come up. Fundamentally, I

[47]

suppose, this is the reason why in the last year or so, every school of education in the country has suddenly turned on and become extremely interested in the intrinsic philosophy and the basic motivation of the Industrial Areas Foundation, and in what is involved in an organization such as B.U.I.L.D.

Part II

RACIAL ISOLATION

IN THE

URBAN COMMUNITY

IMPLICATIONS FOR

THE SCHOOLS

4

SCHOOL SEGREGATION AND DESEGREGATION: SOME MISCONCEPTIONS

DAVID K. COHEN

THERE ARE A FEW misconceptions which always seem to be current in communities seeking to eliminate racial isolation in their schools. Misconceptions do not cause segregated schools, but they do slow the pace of school desegregation. They can help to provoke rather intense community conflict, and often create much anxiety on the part of school superintendents and board members.

They are deceptively simple, and typically are embodied in statements made or questions asked at heated meetings.

First—"why must Negro children attend desegregated schools in order to learn well—why can't education in Negro schools just be improved?"

Second—"schools didn't cause the segregation of students; it is a housing problem, and the schools' business is education, not integration."

Third—"school desegregation is impossible; white parents will withdraw their children from integrated schools because of prejudice, declining academic standards, discipline problems, or the like."

[51]

"Why Can't the Negro Schools Be Improved?"

This question and the misunderstandings which underlie it are the more difficult to deal with because they rest in part on truth, and in part on simplistic ideas of how children learn. Partly true because improved education is necessary and helpful for all children; simplistic because the question assumes that children's academic competence is determined wholly or mainly by the quality of their instruction.

This is precisely what most school systems have assumed in their efforts to remedy underachievement and educational failure in predominantly Negro schools. Existing programs of compensatory education assume that the educational problems experienced by Negro children in racially isolated schools are traceable to the individual "cultural deficiency" of the children, and perhaps to the objective deficiencies of their schools and their teachers. Underachievement and school failure, the schools have argued, can be reversed if the quality of education in predominantly Negro schools is improved. This, it is said, will remedy their historic pattern of inadequacy, and compensates for the educational deficiencies which Negro children usually have when they enter school.

This formulation supposes that the process of education is something that goes on mainly between individual students and their teachers, and that when a child fails it is because he or his teacher is in some way deficient.

Certainly it is true that poor children, regardless of their color, have more difficulty with the verbal and behavioral style of schools than children from more advantaged homes; as presently constituted, the style of schools is best suited to

[52]

middle class children. It is questionable whether it is the style of children or the style of the schools which is deficient, but disadvantaged children do have more difficulty with reading, writing, and achievement tests than children from advantaged backgrounds.[1]

It is also true that the quality of teaching in schools is very important. The Coleman survey—*Equality of Educational Opportunity*—shows this to be the single most important aspect of the educational program schools offer. Regardless of their own background, or the social class level of the other students in their school, children who have better teachers—teachers with strong academic training, high verbal achievement, and a belief that their children can learn—perform at a higher level than those whose teachers are less qualified.[2]

But having said that we must go on to say that there is more to the development of academic competence than what an individual student and an individual teacher bring to the classroom. Programs of educational compensation are based on the notion that there are two critical processes that determine learning: the interaction between parent and student, and the interaction between teacher and student. Yet there is very strong evidence that there is a third set of processes—related to interaction among students—which strongly affects the development of academic competence. For Negro students in urban areas these processes are most evident in the relationship between the social class and racial composition of student bodies, and achievement.[3]

Regardless of color and educational quality, a poor child who attends school with a substantial majority of children from more advantaged homes performs at a higher academic level than a poor child—similarly situated in all other respects—who attends school with a majority of poor children. The U.S. Commission on Civil Rights' study, *Racial Isolation in the Public Schools,* shows that the performance difference for these two "average" students, if they are twelfth graders, can be between one and three grade levels in reading achievement. [4] This is not surprising, in view of the fact that the *Equality of Educational Opportunity* survey showed that the social class composition of student bodies is more closely related to student achievement than any other aspect of schools. [5]

The full explanation for this is surely complex, but at least one of the central principles seems apparent. Increasingly, as they move through the grades, children are open to the influence of their peers. Some of these influences are social, and some academic. A child who attends school with a substantial majority of other children who do not come to school with a good verbal "headstart," who have become convinced that America holds little hope for their success, and whose previous school career is marked by frustration, mediocrity, or failure is not likely to believe that he will succeed in school, to be motivated for such success, or to perform well. Children set the standards for their school performance and measure their educational ambitions in good part against the performance standards and ambitions of their schoolmates.

In addition, there is the simple but important fact that a low-performing school is less intellectually and academically stimulating than a high-performing school. [6]

The social class composition of schools affects children regardless of color, but it has particular implications for

[54]

Negroes. The elimination of social class isolation in city schools would necessarily result in substantial racial desegregation, for there are relatively few middle-class Negro children and relatively few predominantly advantaged predominantly Negro schools.[7] Most urban Negro children in America are poor, and to be in school with advantaged children they would have to be in school mostly with white children.

But quite apart from considerations of schools' social class composition, there is the effect of their racial composition. Negro children who attend school with a majority of other Negro children of a given social class level do not perform as well as Negro children who attend school with a substantial majority of whites of that same social class level.[8]

Why is there such a "racial isolation" effect? There are at least two characteristics of Negro schools which seem to impede effective learning. First, by virtue of being Negro institutions they are stigmatized as inferior by most whites. This stigma of inferiority is communicated to parents, teachers, and students, and it seems to depress their expectations, and the students' performance. Second, they are not schools which can provide Negro students with one very important foundation for success in America—the cumulative experience of achieving in cooperation and competition with whites. And since most Negro children attend schools which are predominantly Negro and predominantly poor, they experience a double disadvantage of class and color.

Examine the results after the end of a child's public elementary school career, in terms of his ninth grade achievement. The average Negro student who has attended school with white children since the early elementary grades, experiences less than half the academic disadvantage of a Negro student who has attended school only with other (disadvantaged) Negroes.[9] Less than one-fifth of the Negro children in the urban centers of the North and West attend school with a majority of white children, and a small proportion of those have attended school with a majority of white children for their entire school careers.[10] Thus, a tiny fraction of the Negroes who attend urban public schools throughout this country attend schools which provide them with a good chance of success. The overwhelming majority leave school academically crippled, with such low levels of academic skill that there can be little hope for them to succeed. The average twelfth grade Negro student in the metropolitan northeast reads below the ninth grade level.[11]

These statistics suggest the need for rapid and massive educational improvement. But such improvement—badly needed as it is—should not be undertaken in a way which misconceives or ignores the effects of the student environment in schools. In schools segregated by color and class the student environment is a barrier to learning; the collective disadvantagement of the student body makes it difficult for effective learning to take place. The programs of educational improvement which so far have been devised do not take account of this, but proceed on the assumption that the problem is the deprivation of individual children. Since they incompletely define the problem—by failing to consider the student environment effects—it is not surprising to find that they have shown no lasting improvement in student achievement.

In this connection the Syracuse, New York schools' experience bears repeating. Dr. Franklyn Barry, School

Superintendent there, said that:

> A year ago we did a study of 24 of the Negro kids that were bussed out from Washington Irving (an all-Negro school). They still were living where they had been, their economic level had not changed, and we matched them with similarly-situated Negro children from Croton (an all-Negro) school. The study covered an eight month period. The bussed children averaged 9.2 months progress in the eight months, without any great supportive help out in their new schools. Those children who were left behind in the de facto segregated school achieved only 4 months—average—for that 8 month period. And Croton is a school saturated with compensatory programs. It proved to the satisfaction of most of our Board that our new thrust had better be in the area of integration rather than compensatory services.[12]

It is possible, no doubt, for such programs to improve achievement if the school organization is so changed that every few students have an individual teacher. Such programs might well be more effective—in the sense of developing academic competence—because sharply increasing the numbers of teachers might sharply reduce the effects of the student environment. But imagine the cost of reducing the pupil-teacher ratio to 5-1 or 8-1; this is to contemplate a revolution in education that no individual school district can afford.

Moreover, the problems that arise from racially isolated schooling are not limited to the development of academic competence. And this brings us to the second misconception.

"This is a Housing, Not a School Problem"

Behind that simple statement is a deceptive and mistaken view of schools' effects on students. Two sets of facts illuminate this confusion.

[57]

First, it is incorrect to say that schools have not directly caused segregation, and to infer from that a lack of responsibility for remedy. Historically, schools have caused or permitted changes in attendance patterns which create, compound, and reinforce racial isolation. This has come about in a variety of ways—intentional and unintentional. In some cases it involved permissive state statutes; in other cases courts have found deliberate gerrymandering; and in many cases, apparently neutral decisions have created and intensified racial isolation.[13]

This category of practices has been important in the past, and in some respects—school construction—is still a major cause of racial isolation in schools. So if direct causal involvement of this sort is required to justify remedy, it exists.

However, this approach understates the role schools play in causing segregation, because it limits consideration of the schools' effect to their impact upon boundaries and the like. But—and this is the second point—schools have a marked impact upon their students' achievement, attitudes, and associations in later life.

School achievement is closely correlated with later economic and occupational achievement; thus one of the effects of racially isolated schooling for Negroes is to reduce their adult occupational and economic achievement. Negro adults who attended segregated schools are less likely to hold white collar jobs or to have substantial incomes than those who attended desegregated schools.[14] Among the factors which inhibit residential desegregation is the low income levels of most Negroes; even if there were effective fair housing laws, only a small proportion of urban Negroes could afford the housing thus open to their occupancy. The academic damage done in schools—which limits Negroes' economic opportunities—thus reinforces Negro poverty and ghettoization. It hardly matters if the damage is inflicted by intent or indifference—the result is reduced economic opportunity and intensified housing segregation.

Therefore, given existing Negro income levels, those who say that integrated schools should wait on integrated housing effectively advocate the maintenance of existing patterns of segregation in housing and schools.

It is even more informative to consider the attitudes and associations of Negro and white adults, as they relate to the racial composition of the schools they attended as children. Those who attended racially isolated schools are likely to express fear, distrust, and hostility toward members of the other race. White adults who attended racially isolated schools are likely to oppose measures designed to secure equal opportunity for Negroes. They are likely to live in segregated neighborhoods, and to express a desire to continue living in such neighborhoods. Their children typically attend all white schools, and they are likely to reject the idea of their children attending desegregated schools.

Likewise, Negroes who attended segregated schools not only are likely to fear and distrust whites, but they are surprisingly likely to express the idea that they would like to get even with them; there are manifestations of this in the cities every summer now. These Negroes are not likely to live in desegregated neighborhoods, and they are likely to hesitate about sending their children to desegregated schools.

[59]

Negro and white adults who attended desegregated schools have a rather different pattern of attitudes and associations. They are more likely to live in desegregated neighborhoods and to have children in desegregated schools. They are likely to express, if they are white, strong support for measures designed to secure equal opportunity for Negroes. And Negroes and whites alike are unlikely to express fear and distrust of—or a desire to get even with—members of the other race.

These differences are taken apart from the particular neighborhoods in which these adults lived as children, and apart from their relative poverty or affluence; we see here chiefly the effect of schools.[15] For example, high-status (college educated) Negroes who attended segregated schools are *less likely* to live in integrated neighborhoods than lower-status (high school educated) Negroes who attended integrated schools.[16]

The data suggest how, as the public schools shape the values and attitudes of children, they also set the mold for their attitudes and associations as adults. As segregated schools create and reinforce preferences for association only with persons of one's own race, they build the foundation for acting out these preferences in adult housing and school decisions.

Here is a second direct way, then, in which the schools cause and compound residential segregation. Efforts to eliminate residential segregation are blocked by the Negro and white attitude barriers created in racially isolated schools. Thus, once again it is clear that those who say that school segregation cannot end until housing segregation does effectively support the maintenance of segregated schools. And those schools will shape the racist attitudes on the basis of which housing will remain segregated for more generations.

So again, if involvement as a causal agent is required to assign schools a responsibility for remedy, such a responsibility exists. It is a serious mistake of fact and judgment to say that this is housing and not a school problem.

This evidence on the later life effects of education also bears on the original misconception about improving schools. Let us assume that compensatory programs will make substantial improvements in Negro achievement. But there is a stronger relationship between schools' racial composition and students' racial preferences than between their academic performance levels and their racial preferences. Students with high levels of academic competence who attend isolated schools are less likely to express a preference for desegregated schools and friends of the other race than those who do less well academically, but attend desegregated schools.[17] Improvements in students' academic competence will not eliminate the schools' contribution to increasing segregation. To focus only on the academic outcomes of education is to misconceive the broad social effects of education. Even if programs of compensatory education could substantially improve academic competence in schools isolated by race and social class, they would continue to intensify and compound segregation and the specifically racial damage it generates for white and black Americans. Negro achievement is no more a remedy for segregation and the racism it produces than white achievement has been in the past.

"If Schools are Desegregated, the Whites Will Leave"

It often has been said that if schools are desegregated white families will march noisily away. They will, it is argued, enrol their children in private schools, move to all-white suburbs, or

[61]

in some other way avoid having their children attend school with Negroes.

Experience, however, shows that this has not been true. School districts in northern and western cities which have desegregated did indeed experience bitter and vocal opposition from white families. Yet in these districts there has been no discernible flight of whites from the public schools. There is no evidence from these cases that school desegregation, effectively undertaken and accomplished, leads to an exodus of whites. These communities had school administrators and school boards that were united on the issue; they approached it as a problem of the total community, carefully worked out a plan, took it to the community for discussion and information—not for a vote—and then implemented it. Opposition subsided, and after a year or two there were few signs of the earlier problems and divisions.

It is not really surprising that school desegregation has been effective where it has been undertaken with commitment and leadership on the part of school authorities. After all, this is only to say that in these communities school authorities led on the issue of school desegregation in the same way that they typically lead on such issues as support of school operating and capital improvement levies.[18] In American education, such informed leadership usually wins.

In these communities white parents learned that their children do not suffer in desegregated schools. The performance of white children on standard achievement tests shows quite clearly that they perform just as well in desegregated schools as white children in all-white schools. Apart from academic performance, there is the simple but terribly important fact that white students in desegregated schools are much less likely to hold racist attitudes. It is such attitude change on the part of whites that is required for a lasting solution to this nation's racial problems.

Of equal interest are the plans which some larger communities have formulated for education parks, or campus schools. Since they would substantially enlarge attendance areas, education parks could provide desegregated schooling in districts where more traditional techniques would not have much effect. By the same token, the consolidation of school resources in such schools would permit substantial increases in educational quality for all children. Studies suggest that the saving on construction-associated costs alone could be as much as 20 per cent over neighborhood schools. They also suggest that very substantial improvements in educational quality for all children could be provided without drastic increases in school's operating budgets. There is good reason to believe that if desegregation and educational improvement for all students are associated in policy and practice, there will not be great problems of community acceptance.[19]

There are a few other misconceptions, of a small order of importance, associated with white anxiety and resistance. It often is said, for instance, that neighborhood schools are sacrosanct and busing evil. Yet over 40 per cent of the nation's public school children ride buses to and from school every day.[20] There has been no outcry about that, for the simple reason that parents see a better education at the end of the bus ride; the demise of the little red school house was associated with educational improvement. There doesn't seem to be any evidence that riding a bus damages children from this segment of the public school population. Indeed, it is worth noting that although there is a considerable amount of literature on how to buy and maintain school buses, and how to recruit and train good bus drivers, there isn't any data on how a bus ride can affect children educationally or psychologically.

Since 1954 there also has been a growing concern about neighborhood schools. Yet the corollary of the 40 per cent plus bus riding figure is that 40 per cent plus do not attend neighborhood schools. As with the alleged evils of busing, one is unable to find out much about the educational advantages of neighborhood schools; there is no data on the subject. There never has been a study of the relationship between childrens' distance from school and the quality of their education and it is doubtful that there ever will be.

There is a final misconception which holds that, if it is ignored, the problem of racial isolation in schools will go away. This is particularly difficult; one can point out the facts about busing or neighborhood schools, but it is not easy to remedy a persistent reluctance to face problems squarely. And this posture is a common one, particularly among the people professionally concerned with education in urban areas. To confirm this all one needs to do is examine the record of statements and action in city schools for the last thirteen or fourteen years. For the most part, educators there appear to have proceeded on the assumption that if they go about business as usual—which includes efforts to improve education by offering more now of what hasn't worked in the past—all the noise will subside. Such attitudes and behavior are untenable on both political and ethical grounds.

Politically the destructiveness of this position is evidenced by the fact that in the older and larger cities the public schools are losing their constituents and clients. Institutions being deserted in this fashion are not healthy. There are a few facts which illustrate this.

First there is the increase in attendance at schools other than the central city public schools. Those who have the economic wherewithal have for some time been withdrawing their children from the central city public schools. In most cases these people are white, but this is not a flight from Negroes. It is a flight from schools which, by comparison with private or suburban public schools, are increasingly poor. Data are available, for example, on Negro and white sixteen- and seventeen-year-olds for 1965. They show no variation for whites in private school attendance by social class. About 15 per cent of the white students—white collar or working class—attend non-public schools. But for Negroes there is a striking difference. Only 1 per cent of working class Negro students were in non-public schools, but over 40 per cent of all the Negro students from white-collar homes were in non-public schools.[2 1] Well-to-do Negroes are voting with their feet against central city public schools, as many whites have been doing for some time.

But turn to less advantaged Negroes; there are other facts which illustrate the schools' loss of constituents. The relevant data here are typified in the history of the dispute over Intermediate School 201, in Harlem, in 1966-1967. This dispute probably marked a turning point, but it has been widely misinterpreted. The impression one is left with from the communications media is that a group of Negro parents suddenly had embraced the doctrine of "black power," and were demanding control of the school on those essentially

[65]

ideological grounds. This was not the case. Many of those parents had been fighting for years to integrate I.S. 201. This was their hope for quality schools, for equal opportunity and improved education. After years of conflict, of promises made by the schools and not kept, these parents finally concluded that the New York City Board of Education was not going to integrate the school. They already know that in all the years of promised integration the children's achievement had not improved. From this loss of hope came the demand that they be given a large voice in the school's operation. This was a result of the parents' growing sense that the school system did not have their childrens' interest at heart, and their conclusion that those closest to the children—Negroes and parents—could not but do a better job. So they demanded control of the school; demanded that it become a publically funded but privately controlled institution.

In all societies institutions and important policies rest in some degree on consent, whatever the political forms and processes may be. In democratic societies the institutions and policies are more directly and regularly related to consent. And the schools, a critically important institution, are being deserted—those who can't affort it financially are trying to accomplish the same aim politically. Even this most rudimentary form of consent and participation is being withdrawn. It is a symptom of a profound loss of confidence in public institutions.

On one level at least the I. S. 201 affair and school enrollment trends both manifest in a quieter way what is evident in the summer urban disorder—a rising sense of deprivation and a declining confidence in the ability and desire of existing institutions to provide improved opportunity. It is

[66]

said that disorders are no reason for action. But far more disturbing than the open disorder in the cities is the disorder in our priorities and sensibilities, which allows us to permit the regular and public emotional and academic devastation of Negro children. That this well-known process goes on year after year is a more troubling comment on our mental health, and on the vitality of public institutions than the riots. It is quite enough reason for action.

There also is an ethical dimension to the view that problems—if ignored—will go away. Ultimately any important social policy rests on an ethical judgment: apart from the routine matters, what public officials do or fail to do rests in part on their judgment as to whether given policy is right or wrong. The view that the problem of racially isolated schools will go away if ignored rests on such a judgment. Simply stated, it is that it is permissible for generations of Negro children to go through the public schools being educationally crippled. Of course, most of these public men and women would say that segregation does no harm, or that the schools Negro children attend are being improved, or perhaps that desegregation is politically impossible. But if these public men and women in urban education were to be ethical, even in the crudest sense—given any one or combination of these responses—they could only enrol their children in the schools which they deem it permissible for Negro children to attend.

One immediately recognizes just how distant a possibility that is, and precisely why it is so distant. This recognition should provoke some sense of just how urgent the need for action is. Urgent for Negroes, who are damned to academic failure by the schools that now exist, and for whites, who must be damned to failure as human beings while what exists is allowed to continue.

[67]

NOTES

1. The best evidence on this derives from James S. Coleman *et al.*, *Equality of Educational Opportunity* (Washington, D.C.:U.S. Government Printing Office, 1966), pp.298-302. A greater proportion of variation in student achievement (among schools) is accounted for by students' social class than any other factor.

2. *Ibid.*, pp.316-19.

3. *Ibid.*, pp.302-25. The Coleman report is only the most recent work in a long tradition of research in this area. For data over time on the same students and schools (and a good review of past work), see A. Wilson, "Educational Consequences of Segregation in a California Community," in U. S. Commission on Civil Rights, *Racial Isolation in the Public Schools* (Washington, D.C.: U.S. Government Printing Office, 1967), II, 165-206. Wilson shows that the cumulative social class composition of students' elementary schools is as closely related to their sixth grade reading achievement as their individual family background; table 17, p.181.

4. U.S.C.C.R., *op. cit.*, I, Figure 1, 80.

5. Coleman *et al.*, *op. cit.*

6. In this connection it is important to notice that these are school-specific processes. Wilson, *op. cit.*, pp.172-82, was able to weigh the relative strength of school and neighborhood context upon achievement, and he found the latter to have no explanatory power. As he points out (p.180), this has important implications for school policy; among them is the fact that changing students' school context is not likely to react negatively upon them due to remaining neighborhood disparities.

7. Only about 20-25 per cent are middle class.

8. See U.S.C.C.R., *op. cit.*, I, Figure 5, 90. See also Vol. II, Appendix C-1, 35-142.

9. U.S.C.C.R., *op. cit.*, I, Figure 6, 107.

10. Estimated from U.S.C.C.R., *op. cit.*, I, 4-5, and Vol. II, Table 2.1, 48. Since the sample in Table 2.1 was drawn to over-represent Negroes in desegregated situations, the figures in the text above must err on the side of overestimating integration.

11. U.S.C.C.R., *op. cit.*, II, Table 4.2,67. The average Negro verbal ability score is actually 3.6 years behind the average white student in grade twelve.

12. Speech by Dr. Franklyn Barry before Ohio Conference on School Desegregation, Akron, June 10, 1967.

13. U.S.C.C.R., *op. cit.*, I, 39-71.

14. U.S.C.C.R., *op. cit.*, I, 108-9.

15. This entire analysis of adult attitudes and associations is drawn from U.S.C.C.R., *op. cit.*, I, 109-13.

16. U.S.C.C.R., *op. cit.*, I, Table II, 113.

[68]

17. D. Singer,"Interracial Attitudes of Negro and White Fifth Grade Children in Segregated and Unsegregated Schools" (Ed.D. dissertation, Columbia University, 1966), chap. III and IV.

18. On this entire subject, see Stout *et al., School Desegregation: Progress in Eight Cities* (Chicago: 1966), especially chaps. IX and XI.

19. U.S.C.C.R., *op. cit.*, I, 167-83.

20. U. S. Office of Education, *Digest of Educational Statistics* (Washington, D.C.: U.S. Government Printing Office, 1965), p.29.

21. Nam and Rhodes, *Inequalities in Educational Opportunities* (Florida: 1966), Table 15.

5

SCHOOL COMMUNITY RELATIONS IN LARGE CITIES

CHARLES E. STEWART

THIS DISCUSSION IS addressed to problems of improving school community relations. It is a topic of great concern to all of us and particularly those of us having some responsibility for the quality of education in those schools that serve large populations of so-called "disadvantaged" children. The term "disadvantaged" is used to describe these children with some hesitancy. I moved' away from the term "culturally deprived" some years ago because it seems rather ridiculous to talk about children as being culturally deprived when we know perfectly well that every child has a culture. He brings it to school with him every day. Let me illustrate this with an incident that occurred when I was a school principal. A first grade teacher was preparing her children for a story hour and, like all good first grade teachers, she was taking time to discuss some of the concepts in the story. This was a story about dragons and fairies, and she wanted to be sure they knew what these creatures were, so she asked the kids in the room, "Now you all know about fairies?" The kids all of course said yes. One little boy said, "There is one living right across the street from me." That is one of the favorite anecdotes that I have collected over the years, and not a joke. Quite often people who hear me using it, usually suburbanites who want to know more about this strange critter called "the disadvantaged child," don't laugh when I tell it. Then, of course, I have to explain to them that it is they who are culturally deprived.

The Racial Factor in School Community Relations

I have some special feelings about school community relations in disadvantaged neighborhoods, and they are derived at least in part from my own experience in the community relations division of a large city school system, and from my experience as a school principal. I hope you will believe me when I tell you that, as a central office person, I found putting out fires started by someone else to be far more difficult than coping with those I started myself as a principal. But while putting out school community fires, in the division of school community relations, I became sharply aware that many problems that we have to deal with were a very direct result of failure to understand the parents whose children we are attempting to serve. I found this to be especially true if those parents happened to be Negro. For example, I recall an incident in which a Negro woman with a daughter in one of our elementary schools was complaining quite vehemently because her child had come home one day in tears saying she had been forced to read a book called *Uncle Tom's Cabin.* Some of the other youngsters in the class had noted a likeness between the child and the picture of Topsy in the book. This made the child tearful, and it brought the mother to school in a rage. The principal of the school couldn't understand what it was all about. In the first place, the book is a classic, and in the second place, these people were from the South. The principal found it

[72]

difficult to understand why somebody who had just left the South didn't appreciate the advantages of being in the North enough to be willing to put up with a thing like an old-fashioned picture of Topsy in the book. This principal found it very difficult to understand that because the woman had left the South, and because she had only been in the North for a very short time, were the very reasons why she was complaining so bitterly. This is an example of the kind of human process that we will encounter as we try to work more and more closely with parents who are not accustomed to our working closely with them. And as we move toward them with outstretched arms saying, "We welcome you into this school enterprise," it's amazing how many kinds of things they are going to do to test whether we really mean it when we say "welcome." It's the same kind of testing out process that we experience with children; but then, people are just like children.

There is no question but what the racial factor often is a very confusing complication in problems which we call school community relations. In this society of ours which is undergoing a very dramatic social and technological revolution, and in the kaleidoscopic events that characterize that revolution, the problems that we sometimes label racial, are really but one aspect of the total pattern of social and technological change. And I think that fact has been obscured too often by our willingness to interpret deep social issues as racial issues. Often these interpretations have limited our educational thinking and planning and restricted them to techniques of defense, conciliation, and compromise. The decisions rooted in some of these expediences of compromise and conciliation more often than not have infringed only on the outer framework of the educational structure, rather than at its core or its processes and the resulting educational arrangement has not always been productive. Now no one would disagree with the position that schools are here to serve the people. They're supposed to serve the needs, the ideas, and the aspirations of this democracy of ours, or as Miller and Spaulding put it, "The schools serve continuously as an agency by which society examines itself and redirects itself in terms of what it determines to be good."[1] The question being raised is, how well do the schools serve in that capacity? The fact emerges that the school serves in that capacity effectively only when the constantly evolving nature of societal needs, ideals, and aspirations are assessed and when creative attempts are made to gear the schools for educational changes dictated by that assessment. In this process, it's important that school people become pretty skillful, certainly as skillful as possible, in developing lines of communication which will yield an accurate assessment, which will yield sanctions for programs and innovation, and which will yield support for program implementation.

I have chosen to emphasize: first, some of the myths about low status people in general, and Negroes in particular—myths which I believe severely get in the way of our understanding of disadvantaged communities; and second, I want to talk about this phenomenon which we refer to as leadership in the Negro community; and third, I want to touch on the role of intermediate leadership and particularly the principal.

Three Myths Concerning Low Status People

Not too long ago a school administrator in my acquaintance, who was a veteran of more than thirty successful years in the business, threw up his hands in frustration and said, "Stewart, I don't know what's happening anymore. There was a time when I knew the Negro community well; I knew its leaders personally. Why they were my personal friends, and now it looks like there is a new leader popping up every day. I find it difficult to understand what it is they want." The dilemma of that school administrator emphasizes the very first point to be made and that is there is no such thing as a Negro community. I'll use the term because it's a convenient way to refer to a group of people, but we are in error to think of Negro people as an undifferentiated order. This is a concept that our perceptions have created for us. But, school administrators largely attempt to operate as if there were, indeed, a Negro community. This issue of ethnic identification was pointed up a long time ago by E. Franklin Frazier in his book *Black Bourgeoise.*[2] While Frazier may have been a little unfair in the way he generalized about what he called middle class Negroes, and particularly about the motivations of these middle class Negroes, I think it only fair to agree that there is a great deal of resentment among many so-called Negro middle class people, which is directed against the low status Negro. Middle class Negroes frequently see the low status Negro as a barrier to their own social mobility. In a more recent study, upper class respondents much more frequently than lower class Negroes, tended to disassociate themselves entirely from ethnic identification, particularly in situations where the racial reference was deemed unfavorable, so that the illusion of a unified Negro community with an understanding and cooperative leadership is really rooted in an era when Negroes could not or dared not without permission, be articulate about their needs and aspirations. And that illusion grew strong by virtue of the limited channels for communicating between whites and Negroes.[3] It is really difficult to say now whether this comforting illusion was created by white people or for them.

The second point of importance to school people is that the human differences which exist within the so-called Negro community are not easily classified. Class and status lines are less clearly drawn and not easily equated with those of the white community. What a Negro does for a living, for example, is not always a reliable clue to his real or perceived status in the Negro community. This can be illustrated very well within the school organization itself. In the Negro community, the teacher historically has enjoyed somewhat higher social status than that of the white teacher in a general community. Important also, though operative on a lesser degree, is the high professional status of the Negro secretary operating in a school setting. The Negro secretary often has a husband who is a business or professional leader in the community and she is often active in community organizations. School administrators who were unaware of this fact have on occasion treated the Negro secretary as if she were just a secretary, only to learn that her firsthand observations of administrative behavior were translated into a real negative kind of imagery, which was transmitted to the so-called Negro community.

An even better example of this is in the bitter complaint I received once from a cleaning woman in one of our schools. She explained that the principal in her building, who was a human relations seeker, often showed his satisfaction for the work done by the custodial staff by giving them a pat on the back or sometimes a pat on the head, or sometimes he would put his arms around their shoulders. According to the complaint, her white co-workers enjoyed this benevolent kind of gesturing. They recognized it as an appreciation for their important roles in the building, but the Negro woman did not enjoy it at all. Now the principal's motives are not in question here. He undoubtedly treated the Negro woman as he did all the other members of the custodial staff. He had no regard for color, or sex, but what he didn't understand was that the Negro cleaning woman didn't perceive herself as just a cleaning woman. In the first place, she was a widow who had seen better days. She was still active in a bridge club, which included some wives of business and professional men. And furthermore, she was president of her local block club, a fact which the principal would have known had he attended any of the meetings.

The third point to be emphasized is that not all those who live in disadvantaged areas are themselves disadvantaged. Most neighborhoods in the Negro community present a very wide variety of home and family circumstances, and the factor of increased mobility in housing does not appreciably alter that picture. It's true that a growing number of Negro families have reached middle class economic status and hold middle class aspirations, but they still cannot easily move out of areas characterized by defamation and neglect. By and large they can move within those areas, but not away from them. Thus, the middle class Negroes, regardless of their higher aspirations and expectations, send their children to the same schools with the disadvantaged children. They are compelled to observe the efforts of our schools in attempting to educate the disadvantaged child, admittedly an area where we are weak. And they denounce us in our efforts because we fail their children too. Much of the denunciation might be avoided were school people better able to understand and deal with this range of differences within and among Negroes.

Contrary to what earlier sociologists taught us, low status Negro parents do not have a negative attitude toward education. Despite all evidence, which would tend to dim their faith, low status Negro parents still believe that education is the way out

[77]

for their kids. They's not joiners; they're not going to come to a PTA meeting to see a travelogue type film, or hear lectures on matters for which they feel no immediate concern. But they are interested in their kids and they can be reached with some down-to-earth approaches which assume that interest. Of course, it goes without saying that the school's approach to parents must be one which reflects a genuine interest in the kids. Too often what has been interpreted as a rejection of education by low status parents is more truly a rejection of the school and its personnel. Many a Negro parent, who has been enticed by the children to attend PTA meetings so their class will win a gold star, will never return again, because of the addiction to this business of first-name calling. Mrs. Dora Jones, who stands on her feet all day doing housework, and who has been called Dora all her life to connote a subservient status, doesn't want to be called Dora when she comes to the school. She wants to be called Mrs. Jones. She's already uncomfortable and insecure in the alien setting of the school, and she's got to be made to feel that she belongs there, that she's important, and that she's welcomed as an important human being. This is not going to be done by the use of gimmicks, like the instant brotherhood that we sometimes think is inherent in first-name calling.

Leadership in the Negro Community

This is the question, or one of the questions that white people ask most frequently: Who speaks for the Negro? And the only truthful answer today, of course, is that no one speaks for the Negro. And if that answer is a little disconcerting, I guess it must be remembered that the question itself is rooted in some clearly obsolete notions about the nature of the Negro

[78]

community. As a matter of fact, it's not certain that any one person ever did speak for all Negroes. But Negroes, until recent years, had but a small voice in determining who their leaders would be, or maybe more aptly put, who would be their spokesman. This was true primarily because the first requirement for a Negro leader was that he be acceptable to the white power structure. Even in recent years, published articles by well-known Negro wirters such as Lomax and Fuller have accused the mainly middle class Negro leadership of being white carbon copies.[4] Adam Clayton Powell, when he was a congressman, spoke to this point rather vigorously in what he called "A Black Position Paper" in Chicago back in 1965. Powell said: "Black communities all over America today suffer from absentee black leadership. This black leadership, the ministers, the politicians, the businessmen, doctors and lawyers, must come back to the Negroes who made them in the first place, or be purged by the black masses."[5] The ex-congressman called on Negroes to reject the white community's carefully selected ceremonial Negro leaders, and insist that the white community dealings be with black community leaders chosen by black communities. Mr. Powell's views on black nationalism may not even today be widely shared throughout the country, but his statements even then reflected a disaffection of the black masses who have not yet felt the effects of true civil rights opportunities. And it is that growing disaffection which provides a platform for the Stokely Carmichaels and the H. Rapp Browns today. It is that growing disaffection which provides the wedges for our professional community organizers such as Mr. Alinsky.

Now it is understandable that the present climate would be favorable to the current thrusts of many individuals in organizations who are striving for leadership in the so-called

[79]

Negro struggle. For in this struggle lies the largest force of power within reach of Negro leaders. Here is power which transcends the boundaries and possibilities of the Negro community alone: It is power that affects the nation. There is a kind of moth-eaten story that went around not long ago. The President was talking on the telephone to Dr. Martin Luther King. His side of the conversation went like this, "Yes, Rev. King. No, Dr. King. Yes, Dr. King. But Dr. King, it's always been called the White House!" This kind of competitive struggle for leadership among Negroes, however, should not be viewed as a kind of tennis game. It's due in part to the basic quest of men for power. And since in the Negro community the greatest source of power is within the Negro struggle, there is fierce competition among men of talent and strength for positions of power. It also meets a deep emotional need within the Negro community. This quest for power is not without precedent. Throughout our history white men of talent and skill have been free to compete for the great fortunes of business, industry, and government leadership, while Negroes have been restricted in this exercise of personal determination and ambition. They now seek and are realizing some of the personal and public rewards of great and powerful positions of leadership.

In spite of this competition it ought to be stated that Negro leadership is far more stable than is generally recognized by the white community. We had a very dramatic illustration of this in Detroit last Thursday. The black nationalist group which were calling themselves the New Black Establishment in the aftermath of the riots in Detroit, held a rally which was attended by all of the militants and the discontents and the malcontents. Also in attendance was the executive secretary of the NAACP, which is not now considered by any means a militant group. It was amazing to hear a young attorney, who is probably the most articulate and the most vociferous of the militants, get up and speak about the need to purge the middle class Negroes who are too soft and too comfortable, who are not pulling their weight. He was wildly cheered by the gallery. Then the NAACP executive secretary got up and spoke and pointed out the need to avoid divisiveness and diversionary activities within the so-called Negro community. He, too, was wildly cheered by the same people. This to me is a very hopeful and very healthy sign that the Negro leadership game is not quite the bouncing ball that it sometimes appears to be. Dan Thompson's study of the Negro leadership class provides an interesting rationale which underlies the need for different organizational approaches within a community.[6] Some organizations and/or individuals meet the need for organizing and planning within the Negro community while others serve more effectively in the give and take process of negotiating across community lines.

In this discussion of leadership a special word has to be said about an emerging breed of middle class Negroes. It is interesting to me that the desires and frustrations of this new breed have become much more acute with the quickening pace of pressures for change both within and without the Negro community. Both the desires and the frustrations are fed by an unrelenting hope for achieving every particular of American middle class respectability and acceptance. Historically, this hope has been as much a source of strength as it has a source of weakness in the Negro cause. On the one hand, it was a stirring for change generated mainly by middle class expectancies which constituted the most persistent and consistent force in the civil rights movement. The financial contributions of middle class Negroes provide the main support for civil rights organizations and particularly the NAACP. On the other hand, it is precisely because their middle class positions place them in a greater vulnerability and risk that the civil rights movement has been up to now so very well disciplined. That this picture is changing is evident in the violence in the cities around the country, and I think these events illustrate the increasing demand on the resources of the trained middle class Negro. These events also illustrate an increasingly responsiveness to the demand to stand up and be counted with his lower class brothers whom he has shunned for so long. Against the background of this changing picture, the Negro teacher stands with other white collar workers in bold relief. He epitomizes in growing measure what Bennett, in *The Negro Mood* calls development of a new self-conception in the Negro psyche, and the growth of a revolutionary will to dignity.[7] And it is in this changing scene that today's administrators must shape new roles out of new understandings and new insights.

The Role of Intermediate Leadership

The administrative structure in the United States is unique, particularly in its designation of the local school district as the locus of responsibility and control. By-passing the controversial advantages and disadvantages of this phenomenon, suffice to say here that one effect is to constrict the population limits in which conflicts in values must be reconciled, agreement on purpose reached, and interpretations of rules made. There is some evidence that the nature of the population has a distinct bearing on the nature of the decision-making processes by which community expectations are translated into educational arrangements. David Minar, at Northwestern University's Center for Metropolitan Studies, explored this assumption by examining some forty-eight suburban school systems around the Chicago area.[8] His investigation was based on the premise that the school system is a form of political system and that such aspects of politics as the forum of the political process, its content of policy, and the character of its output are related in several ways to the culture and structure of the society in which it is imbedded. In this instance we are talking about the local community.

Dr. Minar hypothesized that the American political culture seeks the suppression of conflict, so he compared these forty-eight school community microcosms of the American political culture by their differential successes in reaching the goal of conflict suppression. His study indicates that the principal aspect of social structure which explains aggregate community behavior toward the schools is a status factor. That is to say, the presence in the system of larger proportions of people with high incomes, educations, and occupations, relationships between styles and decision-making at the career level and in school system institutions show theoretically analogous patterns. In districts of relatively low conflict, school boards usually appear to give their superintendents wide latitude in initiative and decision-making while in the high conflict, low resources systems, board members and other functionaries seem to have more power independent of the superintendent. What he is saying in simple terms is that the high status community tends to give to its school authorities a wider range of sanction and freedom in deciding what's to be done and how to do it. These are what he calls high resources, and he finds that in the high resources areas there is low conflict between the school as an institution and its clientele. Conversely, in the low status school systems, that is, where the majority or the predominant population is low status, there tends to be high conflict and a more narrow range of latitude and initiative in decision-making processes.

[83]

Minar's interpretation of school community behavior finds considerable support in the literature dealing with our subcultural differences., characteristics, and value orientations. I point, for example, to an urban study of sixty-seven life-style characteristics which show marked contrast between middle-class American groups and so-called disadvantaged groups.[9] In the category of personal characteristics, I noted several which seemed directly applicable to the point under discussion here. Middle class people put a great emphasis on community, church clubs, and group membership. Disadvantaged people tend to be more individualistic and self-centered, both in their concepts and in their concerns. They are apparently more concerned about how they're going to get along from day to day. The concern shown for immediate problems takes precedence over involvement in broadly organized community activities. Middle class people feel very deeply about their freedom to determine their own life and goals. They feel that they have power over their destiny and a measure of control over what happens to them. Disadvantaged people also want to control their own destiny but tend to be a little more fatalistic. In some instances they lean to group action, and this is not contradictory to what I said earlier, because I mean lean to group action to obtain personal goals. Middle class people are pretty much routine seekers; they are self-assured. Disadvantaged people tend to be action seekers and they carry a constant sense of anxiety. Another interesting point is that middle class people are oriented to progress without too much concern as to methods employed, for example, in business dealings. By contrast, disadvantaged people are oriented to existence.

The tendency in the so-called high status community to be concerned mainly with broad manners of educational policy formation has advantages and disadvantages. There is freedom on the one hand to be innovative, but there is also the possibility of avoiding change for fear of rocking a comfortable boat. School boards and superintendents who have responsibilities for inner city schools don't have any alternatives. Change is imperative. The big question is how to accomplish orderly and productive change in the absence of the kind of consensus which seems to form more easily around the needs and expectations of middle class neighborhoods. I think the answer lies in the talents of that important echelon of leadership which operates between the superintendent and the teacher. For notwithstanding the responsibility of the board and its top administrators, the crucial reflections of the school system's image are seen by most people within the practices of the local schools. There will continue to be need for the development of broad understandings which result from study and planning by city-wide citizens committees. These committees are sincerely committed and when meaningfully engaged they can be of great value especially for consultation and feedback and they can be very valuable as a base for community support for school action of one kind or another. But the local schools are where the action is. It is there that education becomes most real for that particular segment of the community. It is between the local unit and its own service area that we need a more meaningful dialogue.

Few people find great fault with broad concepts of educational function and purpose. Most disagreement, most conflicts, occur at the point where the local school must translate broad societal purposes into those many operational goals which serve as guides to the concrete programs and services. Myron Leiberman in *Future of Education* said, "Every pressure group is for the general welfare and each has its own version of what educational measures do indeed promote the general welfare."[10] So while a school system must be conscious of and responsive to the pressures of the groups, they must also continue to build bridges to a broader base of support and direction which derive from the reciprocal understandings of a local school unit with its own service area. Sound educational practices demand some consideration of differences among various segments of the community. But no school is an island, and no matter how unique its clientele may seem, differences apparent in any one segment of the community must be considered in relation to the total community. And what's more important, perhaps, to the extent that practices differ in one part of the community from those in another, there will be the problems of understanding what are ends and what are means in the educational enterprise.

Communication at the Local School Level

Dialogues to insure maximum understanding of ends and means in education can go on best at the local school level. Such dialogues cannot take place easily in an autocratically oriented administrative structure. In such a situation the local school has relatively little of importance to say to its community. In such a situation there is the constant danger that the real dialogue inevitably will move upward along the hierarchy to where things of importance can be said and heard. When the dialogue occurs at the superintendent or board level, parents and particularly disadvantaged parents, will feel that they need more power. Consequently, they seek help from more broadly based community organizations. In my opinion, many otherwise purposeless community organizations would go out of business if we at the local school level would talk to parents and not push them up this hierarchical line. It's ridiculous, for example, that a parent coming into a school building to visit a classroom, can't have enough dialogue with the principal to understand either why the principal didn't want her to visit that day, that time, or just why she couldn't visit. Why should a matter like this have to end up as a special agenda item before the board of education with two or three attorneys and a whole community organization representing the parent that wanted to visit the classroom? This is a very simple illustration of what I'm talking about. If you can't deal with them at the local level, you push them up the hierarchy. And they will not go to the superintendent and the board without some help. Where they get help is immaterial to them. They'd just as soon get it from a black power group as from their urban leagues. They might even prefer the black power group. More school community conflict could be prevented or resolved closer to the local school level if good two-way lines of communication were maintained between the local school and the community.

In suburbia, such dialogue occurs much more easily and much more continuously through a network of informal personal contacts, letters, and bulletins which are sent home, and parent-teacher organizations which often are related closely to other lines of community power. The local school principal is usually well-known, acceptable, and trusted by parents whose level of personal security and other life-style factors enable them to place confidence in the professional educators. Not so in the inner city where the contacts are few, parents are wary, and feel powerless. Communications often do not reach home and when they do, too often they are not read or fully understood because of the language we use. It is entirely possible for the inner city school to develop a desirable and productive interaction with its community but admittedly it is much more simple not to bother. In this connection just let me say one word about teachers.

It has been said rather often that social pathology among suburbia's children is a direct reflection of the high anxieties and the too high expectations, and the intense competitive style of middle class parents. These same factors influence the parental relationships of outer city school parents with their teachers. Informal relationships of middle class parents with their teachers are particularly subject to influence by the fact that these parents have ready and direct access to the teacher. And access is aided by the fact that the suburban teachers more frequently live where they teach. In contrast, inner city parents have to put forth a very real effort to see their teachers, who for the most part flee the neighborhood when the last bell rings. In the more formal arrangements for teacher-parent contacts like PTA, there are some other kinds of interesting differences between the inner city and the outer city. Middle class parents are usually more content to attend PTA meetings where the main fare is a lecture on how to detect cancer of the breast or color slides of an exciting canoe trip up the Niagara River. This is meaningful entertainment for them, and they're free to enjoy it because of reassuring report cards and their frequent informal conferences with teachers. Inner city parents, on the other hand, want programs showing their children in action. They want to know how well the kids are doing, or why they "ain't." Contrary to prevailing mythology, inner city Negro parents are not indifferent to school affairs and pupil performance. They are, however, not attracted by most of the trivia that fills up PTA meetings.

I have seen middle class parents with teachers in what we call room-parent groups. I have seen middle class parents who have worked together for a whole school year, meeting once a week around discussions of child development theories. They have stimulating discussion, gallons of coffee, and the two together keep these groups interested and intact throughout a school year. Inner city parent interest could never be sustained in the same manner. Most of them would not have returned after the first or second meeting. But I have seen parent groups in the inner city develop some very real interest and commitment to child development and curriculum when the teacher provided the vehicle by which the parent could become actively involved in an inductive process from which the concepts emerged.

Program Changes for Advantaged and
Disadvantaged Children

Schools have missed an excellent opportunity to effect some very real and important program changes under the cover of the crusade for disadvantaged children and the civil rights struggle; changes incidentally which for some time now have been indicated by this dramatic socio-technological revolution that we're involved in. We worked hard at modifying curriculum patterns and materials to make them more suitable for disadvantaged children. We've done so, I suspect, knowing all along that our traditional programs are not entirely suitable for advantaged children either. Fortunately, advantaged parents have not yet discovered this fact. This brings to mind the story of the two first grade children who were talking during recess. They were having a highly stimulating conversation about a rocket ship and one was asking the other something about a new fuel that was going to work wonders and he asked the other kid what he thought about it. The other kid said, "Well, gee. I don't know. I think it depends on the effects of radiation in the substratosphere." Just then the bell rang and the kids had to go in and the first one said, "Shucks, now we've got to go in and string beads." Then there is the report card from the suburban teacher who added a little note that read, "Your son is doing very well except he has too much imagination which must be curbed."

I wonder what's going to happen when middle class white parents find out that their kids produce more real underachievement than do disadvantaged children. I think if they knew this they would insist upon less rigidity in our school programs. Among many other things, they certainly would demand a greater degree of personalization of standards and materials; they's seek reform and maybe even a little vengeance for our having cheated their children for so long.

Oddly enough, if middle class parents demanded these things, Negro parents would accept their word and would want them also because one of the things that plaugues us in working with disadvantaged kids is that Negro parents want what they think is wonderful out there somewhere beyond the walls of their ghetto. If Latin is out there then it must be good for our kids; give us Latin. We can't speak English, but give us Latin. The use of multiple textbooks is a perfect illustration of this. Disadvantaged parents don't want watered down textbooks. They interpret multiple text adoptions, where you use three or four different reading books which vary in difficulty, as a watering down process. They charge us with lowering our standards. They want what's used out there at the type of school where 80 per cent of the kids go to college. The point is they need it out there, too. They just haven't found out yet.

If we could somehow get smart enough to do this reform across the board, this business of working with disadvantaged kids could have reciprocal benefits for all of us. We talk about individualized approaches to reading in our disadvantaged neighborhoods and parents get mad because they think we're trying to sell them something different, and by inference, something infereior. Basically, very little has been prescribed as desirable for disadvantaged kids that's not good for all children, from Head Start to community college. It's not simply a matter of programs of vocational education so there will be a place for nonacademic youngsters; it's a matter of revamping the entire high school program to bring it more nearly in line with the realities of today's world. Instead of worrying only about how to teach about Africa or Negro history, we ought to be concerned about the total social studies offered for all children. More flexibility in organization, more creative teaching, more individualization of materials and more emphasis on learning how to learn, ought to be the order of the day in schools, period!

Racial issues have resulted in a critical scrutiny of our schools; and, if these issues have helped school people take a hard look beyond the racial issues, they will have been valuable beyond any intent of the civil rights groups. I want to conclude by repeating something that Albert Schweitzer observed once: "No ray of sunlight is ever lost, but the bean which it wakes needs time to spout, and it is not always granted to the sower to live to see the harvest. All work that is worth anything is done in faith." I have faith that today's emphasis on improving education for disadvantaged children is the seed which will bear fruit for all children. I have no hope that these disadvantaged youngsters with their own culture, their own style, and their own poverty can help us change the middle class. But I'm certain with growing awareness that if we examine school offerings for inner city kids, we're going to find thruths and consequences which are equally applicable in outer city and suburbs. If we can capitalize on this opportunity for broad improvements in education, then I think Dr. Conant's discovery of disadvantaged children, indeed, will have been a blessing in disguise.

NOTES

1. Van Miller and W. B. Spaulding, *Public Administration of American Schools* (2d ed.; Cleveland: World Pub. Co., 1958).

2. E. Franklin Frazier, *Black Bourgeoise* (Glencoe, Ill.: The Free Press, 1957).

3. Charles E. Stewart, "Controversial Issues Confronting Large City School Administrators," *Urban Education*, I, No. 4 (1965).

4. Louis Lomax, *The Negro Revolt* (New York: Harper & Row Pub., 1962).

5. Adam Clayton Powell, Speech from "A Black Position Paper," Chicago, May 19, 1965.

6. Daniel Thompson, *The Negro Leadership Class* (Englewood Cliffs, N.J.: Prentice-Hall, Inc., 1963).

7. Lerone Bennet, *The Negro Mood* (Chicago: Johnson Pub. Co., 1964).

8. David Minar, *Educational Decision-Making in Suburban Communities: School Board and Community Linkages* (U.S.O.E., 1965 ERIC–ED001400).

9. J. Irwin and C. Irwin, *A Comparative Study of Certain Basic Differences, Characteristics, and Value Orientations Held by The American "Middle Class" With Those Held by Those Classified as Disadvantaged* (Detroit: Wayne State University Press, 1966).

10. Myron Leiberman, *The Future of Public Education* (Chicago: University of Chicago Press, 1960).

6
INTERNAL ACTION PROGRAMS FOR THE SOLUTION OF URBAN EDUCATION PROBLEMS

MARIO D. FANTINI

THIS PAPER WILL FOCUS upon your role as strategists inside the educational establishment and of the need for developing a strategy for reform. The opinions and personal perceptions of what's happening in urban education that I will present to you are based on my personal observations and experiences as a person who has been both inside and outside the system. I'm using as my main laboratory New York City. The premise is that New York City, as a laboratory, gives us an insight in terms of coming attractions and of the implications that these happenings may have for other major American cities. As I see it, it's just a matter of time before all urban centers will be faced with similar problems.

But because you have this time, it gives you a chance to gain from the experience in New York and Philadelphia, and some of the other large cities where the problem is serious. This is why I'm talking to you as strategists.

A Position of Defensiveness

It is very evident that educators and the establishment as a whole are taking a position of defensiveness in response to the charges from the community on the inadequacies of the

[93]

schools. This position is natural because educators are being attacked from all sides. But there's one point that should be made concerning this position of defensiveness. Although it's a human thing, a natural thing to be defensive, educators are consuming energy in the wrong way. Educators should be looking beyond; they should be capitalizing on the crisis situation by assuming a position of leadership which is rightfully theirs. Otherwise, this position of leadership and responsibility will be relinquished to other sources.

There are two fundamental problems facing educators today:

1. The problem of initiating change in urban education on a mass scale.
2. The problem of determining what direction this change should take.

An evaluation of the kinds of programs we have been promoting for the past ten years and which the Ford Foundation has helped to support leaves us no alternative but to suggest that they are not working. I'm referring now to compensatory education. The present system of diagnosing the problem of urban education in terms of individuals who are not making it by any standard and then mounting a program of rehabilitation of the casualty, which is compensatory education, is not doing the job it was designed to do. The assumption that a program of concentrated remediation can make up for the deficiencies in a person's educational development so that the person can fit the educational process is not valid. This rehabilitative strategy is no longer going to be tolerated by the people who are footing the bill. The federal government, which is giving a billion dollars under Title I is raising fundamental and justified questions. Is the program working? What are we getting for it? Is there a payoff?

There is also another strategy which we have entered into and that is so-called desegregation or integration. People in the inner city look at integration in a very interesting way. Namely, that integration seems to be an establishment position, the same as compensatory education. We really don't have massive integration. We can't call what we're doing integration. At best it's small examples of intermixing. Parents in the inner city don't think it's going to come about anyway. They don't feel they can wait for it to happen. Certain minority groups don't feel that integration is an issue. The Puerto Ricans, for example, have their own cultural identity and they want to retain it. Integration to them means assimilation. They feel that what the establishment wants to do is make them look more like us.

The Movement Toward Greater Community Control

The inadequacies of the present system are causing a movement for greater local control. The community is demanding an opportunity to have a greater voice in decision-making in an effort to make the schools more responsive to the needs and aspirations of the community. Parents are demanding quality education which in the inner city is simply defined as the ability to read and write like everyone else. They want their children to be proficient in the three R's. That's the operational definition as people in the ghetto understand it, but their kids are failing and they are demanding an explanation.

The answer they get from the school is that there's something wrong with the environment. They're told that their children are disadvantaged. How do you get up as a professional person and speak to the parents and say that their children are

[95]

disadvantaged? They're not willing to accept this anymore. This is what they're calling "establishment jargon." This is what's happening in New York. We have a lot to learn from these incidents. It's the job of the school to educate everyone. The teachers have been trained to perform this function. These are public schools and the community intends to hold the schools accountable for performing its responsibility to their children.

In short, they're saying, "We can't afford to have our children fail. Education is too important for mobility and everything else. We want to have a greater voice in determining policy."

The impact of this movement has been felt by legislators in New York State. In March, 1967 a law was passed pertaining to New York City which directed the mayor to develop a plan for decentralization of the schools. Without a doubt, this is going to be a new movement in urban education. At the same time, what little movement there was toward integration has begun to filter down resulting in a conflict over which course of action to follow. Some groups are trying to do something in metropolitan planning in an attempt to bring about racial integration while others are seeking a policy of self-determination in an effort to bring the schools back to the community. This group seeks to develop a notion of public accountability, where parents and community become a partner with the educator.

However, there are very few indications of school-community partnership in New York City at the present time. Instead, there is alienation—a complete breakdown in terms of trust. This is not the case in all sectors of the city, but this is happening in those sectors which we refer to as the ghetto: the Puerto Rican community and the Negro community.

In conjunction with this movement within the urban community there is a growing movement from within the profession itself—a movement which is attempting to strengthen the position and security of the professional educator. Certification requirements are being increased and there is rejection of the attempt to assign teaching responsibility to non-certified individuals. This movement has lead to a monopoly by the professional of the public schools—not in a conscious, deliberate way, but in a natural way. Parents feel that the professionalization, the regrouping on the part of the educators, has forced them to react in a militant manner in order to be heard. They feel that they have no one to whom they can appeal in an acceptable manner. The parents of I.S. 201 in New York City, for example, reacted by boycotting the school. This group has for over a year pointed to the deficiencies of the professional. Their appeals to the mayor have been met with charges from the professionals that they are using political influence. Their appeals to the principal are met with the response that they are disadvantaged. They feel they have no alternative but to express their concerns in means that are degrading since more acceptable approaches have met with rebuke.

The parents want action, but they're not getting it. They refer to the Board of Education and the Central Board as the "Board of Miseducation." Educators respond by saying that the community doesn't understand the problems in the school and that the community would not know how to effectively utilize a greater voice in policy-making. Parents respond with charges that the situation could not be any worse than it is now with the professionals in control. There is evidence of a growing sense of alienation between the school and community in which people are forced to take a position rather than to remain neutral. Coalitions are being formed, again, the battlefield model. Parent groups are trying to form a coalition with the teachers against the supervisors. These are the kinds of forces that are being shaped and it can only lead to some kind of conflict. The whole notion of partnership and cooperation is really the rhetoric of textbooks.

The new mission for education is related to the manpower need of society. Education is that important. The rhetoric of the thirties is the reality of today. But educators haven't been equipped for this. The more they close ranks to meet the growing concern and the growing articulation of the parents and of the politicians—because the self-interest of politicians is being served by education—the more we move toward the inevitable conflict.

This is the situation in New York. It may be different in other cities. Philadelphia, for example, may be nipping it in the bud. But the changes in Philadelphia have come about as the result of action on the part of a local board which chose a former mayor to stimulate change. Parents are beginning to reject the concept of professionally dominated schools. In their opinion the public schools are not public at all. Many people have extreme feelings about this. Professor Kenneth Clark talks about the professional monopoly of schools from a sociological viewpoint. He proposes to break the system by opening up competitive sectors in education. He thinks defense should run a sector of an urban school system. Business and industry should run another sector, and universities another. In his opinion, the only way to change education is by breaking the professional monopoly in the schools. Educators may not like it, but this is what is being said.

Another criticism being expressed is that the educational system is falling of its own weight. It's ponderous. The system came out of another century and it's outdated. The purposes of education that are being articulated on the one hand have nothing to do with the operational definition. Quality education for all, universal higher education, etc. are merely expressions and have nothing to do with what really happens because the professional states implicitly that only those who meet specific standards are allowed to continue. Only those who are ready, go ahead. The concept of quality education for all is being misconstrued on the part of the community to mean equal educational attainment for all. The strategy of compensatory education is a natural outgrowth of this attempt to equalize the educational attainment of all children. It is contrary to the notion of individual differences and it raises fundamental questions concerning our philosophy of education.

The public has a right to state the goals of education and to expect the professional to implement procedures that will bring about the achievement of these goals. This is what is being done, but the final evaluation leaves no doubt that the goals are not being accomplished. The community is demanding an accounting and they are not willing to accept the notion that their children are disadvantaged, deprived, or different. The community expects the school to carry out its responsibility to the children and if it can't be done under the present system, they're going to change the system. That's the challenge, the battlefield. It's made both groups more defensive and led to a breakdown of trust and increased alienations. But the energy which is being wasted on defensiveness should be used instead in an effort to develop a new approach to the problem. This is why meetings like this are important. Efforts have to be made to form ties from the inside to the outside before it's too late to create mechanisms to bridge these alienated publics.

The St. Louis Plan

In St. Louis there is a proposal to unify or centralize the city and suburban schools into a metropolitan district, not for the purpose of forcing integration, but for the purpose of creating economy through centralization of services. The next step is to break the system into smaller units in an effort to retain a measure of diversity and autonomy within the larger framework. A central board is simply not equipped to be responsive to the needs of the various groups within the community. Diversity is a goal. It's something we believe in in this country and our educational system should be responsive to this ideal and give it nurturance. This movement would provide for the creation of local school boards that are truly representative of the communities. They could shape the institution to fit the aspirations of the community. In effect, this would mean the creation of local boards of education existing within the larger framework who would have the authority to select their own chief school officers, who would then be responsible for selecting building administrators for the schools under their jurisdiction both from lists of individuals currently in the system and from those now outside the system. This program would tend to play havoc with the reward system as it now exists in large cities. Those who have spent a major portion of their career establishing themselves, would now find their positions jeopardized.

This movement would also tend to make the decision-makers those closest to the learner rather than those farthest removed. It would mean a strengthening of the role of the teacher and the parent. Organizational procedures that would make these agents much more potent than they are now are being sought.

The role of the central office and board would be retained. It would serve to coordinate the activities of the various units, provide incentive grants to foster integration, and carry out long-range planning.

The role of the chief school officer serving one of the communities would be altered to serve as a community planner for education. He would work with the police department, welfare, and recreation officers to coordinate a program of human service. This is a completely new definition of the role of the administrator who previously served in the capacity of chief instructional agent. Consideration is being given to the possibility of releasing teachers on a daily basis to work in teams—not team teaching, but team planning—so that they may participate in making decisions about how the school should be organized for more effective instruction. Thought is also being given to the creation of a new position of instructional leadership. The person occupying this position would serve as a training officer and possibly be selected by the teachers themselves based on his performance and capabilities as an instructor. Hopefully, this would make the instructional program being offered more responsive to the needs of the local community.

We have then the beginning of a bottom-up movement—organic is the word that best describes it—where the agents closest to the learner have more of a voice in the development of the instructional program and those farthest removed become the facilitators and coordinators. The notion of competition within the system is receiving more emphasis and this coincides with the idea of local boards responsive to individual communities within the larger system. The idea of subsystems created to foster research and development will encourage movement and change.

Educators as Leaders and Initiators of Change

The idea that the school should be a place that educates only children is being replaced with the notion that schools should educate people of all ages, and not just on weekdays but evenings, weekends, and summers. People are beginning to ask for the community school that educators have supported with lip-service for such a long time.

Mention was made earlier of various new roles that are emerging. One of these roles concerns the employment of para-professionals. At one stage in the war on poverty we were going to solve our problems by giving everyone a position as an aide or an assistant. In some of these experiments it was found that these assistants were quite effective in achieving results with inner city children—more effective in some cases than the trained specialists. The new careers movement is here to stay and it's a movement to which educators should give some thought because if they don't, it will be done by others who know very little about what goes on in schools.

Politicians are also beginning to take a closer look at what's happening in education. An office of educational liaison has been created in New York City which reports to Mayor Lindsay on the activities in the field of education. The purpose of this office is to establish a system of communication between City Hall and the Board of Education. The same thing is happening at the state level between the commissioners and urban systems.

This is being proposed in Philadelphia and some of the larger urban centers. This liaison role is being coupled with the notion of program budgeting: relating costs to program objectives.

The demands being made by teachers for pay increases create considerable controversy in the ghetto community. The Puerto Rican community cannot understand how a teacher can be rewarded an increase in salary regardless of whether the students pass or fail. In Puerto Rico the professor was responsible for teaching children. If they didn't, there was an accounting. In New York City salaries are being raised $600.00. Yet in some schools, over 80 per cent of the children are failing. This is something they cannot understand.

The attack on the schools will not stop at the public school level. It will be enlarged to include the universities and teacher training institutions. Teachers are telling the parents that the methods they are using to teach children are the methods they were taught at the university. Teachers say that it's possible to do everything right in terms of acceptable proven procedures and still have the children fail. Doctors are professional people. It is possible for a doctor to perform surgery, do everything correctly, and have the patient die. But the parents' response is, "Yes, but if 80 per cent of the patients died, I think you'd raise some questions about the approach."

This is the kind of dialogue that is occurring between the school and the community and the feelings that are developing are not going to be appeased by rhetoric. The people want action. The children are failing and all they can get from the school is rhetoric.

The charge is being made that the curriculum is not even relevant—that it's not linked to any career pattern at all. Graduates are not equipped to go into a career role in business or industry and the implication is that preparation for work is the responsibility of the school. Educators may not agree but some feel it is and that the program should begin early.

Parents are also reacting to the charge by the school people that they are not satisfactorily performing their role as parents. Some feel that the school has a responsibility to teach people how to perform this role satisfactorily since it apparently requires skill and knowledge of child development. Where does a person learn how to be an adequate parent if not in school? It apparently can't be left to chance as it has in the past, since a lack of skill can be and is detrimental to the educational development of the child.

Still other questions are being asked about cybernetics and computerized instruction. Reference is made to the possibility of having a three-part school or a four-part school where one sector is devoted to reading skills, still another to the affective parts of learning, and another purely to intellectual ideas and concepts. People are getting very curious about these new techniques in education which hold so much promise for the future. They want these opportunities for their children and they want them now. The question is, what is the educational establishment going to do about it and when? The changes that are occurring now are being made as a result of pressure being exerted by power sources outside the educational establishment. Educators are being forced to change and somehow I feel that it's time the educators took a position of leadership and initiated change on their own. In what direction should you move? The basic strategy today is institutional reform. You've tried changing the basic purpose of education. It can't be done. You've tried changing the product to fit the process, but it hasn't worked. It's about time you tried to change the process. You're the engineers of that process. It's your responsibility to do it. It's going to take a lot of initiative and drive and hard work and you will face a great many barriers, but the challenge is real and the reward is great. A little tinkering carried on in the form of role playing is not going to be enough. It's not going to solve the problem.

Massive change is needed inside the system and it's your job to divert the energy currently being consumed on defensive maneuvers to measures that will bring about reform and revitalization throughout the organization. It may be too late for New York, but there still may be time for cities like Buffalo where a group of administrators really take the initiative. You're going to have to seek the support and cooperation of the community. If you don't take the initiative somebody else will and then you will have to follow, not lead. And the consequences for the learner will be more severe. The power sources outside the educational establishment are not going to wait much longer. That's clear, and it's been clear for a long time. Administrators have a responsibility for being the initiators of change rather than the protectors of the system. This is what administration is all about.

Part III

SCHOOLS FOR THE

URBAN COMMUNITY

NEED FOR

CHANGE

7

INSTRUCTIONAL PLANNING FOR THE URBAN SETTING

SAMUEL SHEPARD, JR.

THE BANNEKER DISTRICT, located in the city of St. Louis, has achieved some recognition in terms of its ability to develop a program which has proven effective in improving the educational achievement of children from the ghetto. Some of our ideas, experiences, and activities may perhaps provide you with a different point of view, a different insight into your own situation. Some of these ideas may prove applicable to your own situation and be as effective in helping you achieve your goals as they have been to us.

The Banneker District

The St. Louis school system, which includes approximately 150 public elementary schools, is divided into six geographical units. Each of these units is administered by a team consisting of an assistant superintendent in charge and three supervisors; one supervisor works with grades K-2, another 3-5, and the third with 6-8. In addition, we have two consultants, one in music and one in physical education. The offices of each team are located in one of the schools in the district. My position is assistant superintendent in charge of the Banneker district. My office and those of the supervisors and consultants are located in the Banneker Elementary School. The Banneker district is located in the inner city—the "slum area" that so much is being written about. It takes in all of the downtown area and fans out from the big department store center to the run-down commercial area, where people live over and in the rear of stores, and to the brokendown slum residential area. There are twenty-two schools in the district with approximately 15,000 students and 500 teachers. About 98 per cent of the students and 90 per cent of the teachers are Negro. One of the three supervisors and three of the principals are white.

The Banneker district is the poorest of the six districts any way you look at it. No one investigates to determine whether the youngsters who live in our area are eligible for Head Start. This means that the annual family income is under $3,000. As a matter of fact, the annual family income in three schools is under $2,000.

In 1954, St. Louis was a totally segregated city. Immediately after the Supreme Court decision in May, 1954, our Board of Education voted to desegregate the schools. They did this in three steps. In September, 1954, all of the special education facilities and the two teachers colleges were integrated. The following January the secondary schools were integrated, and in September the elementary schools were integrated. At that point, 75 per cent of the students in the Banneker district were Negro.

The problems of de facto segregation is as great in St. Louis as it is in most other American cities. This past year our Board of Education wrote to the superintendents of the twenty-nine school districts in the surrounding suburban communities asking them to make some of their vacant seats available to inner city Negro children. The response has been negligible.

[110]

Quality education cannot be achieved as long as there is racial isolation in the schools. I would like to make that crystal clear. We live in a multiracial, multi-ethnic society. If the goal of education is to prepare children for effective citizenship in a democratic society, then we cannot justify educating them in isolation because it is contrary to the accomplishment of that goal. Efforts are being made to eliminate segregation but the results are pretty poor. The drive to achieve quality education should begin with the elimination of racial isolation in the schools, but the concentration of large masses of Negroes in urban centers has made this extremely difficult to accomplish. We realized that the problems of segregation were not going to be solved immediately, therefore, we decided to do the best possible job of educating our youngsters under existing conditions. We knew we couldn't stand by and wait for this problem of racial isolation to be solved. Too much was at stake in the lives of these youngsters and for their parents. More can be done when the battle has been won, but it has to be won first.

Dr. Conant, in his book *Slums and Suburbs,* saw the present events in his mind's eye and since that time we've benefited from his insight. He expressed concern over what he referred to as the social dynamite that was ready to explode in the big cities of America. He was right. There has been an explosion and I suspect it's going to get worse before it gets better. The intellectual standing of Joe Louis was not held in high regard, but following one of his victories in the ring he made an interesting comment that has relevance to the movement of whites away from the inner city. When asked, "How do you feel when you have to chase your opponent around the ring?" he replied, "They can run, but they can't hide." This is the way I see our situation. White America is running hard, but I don't think it can hide. The white race is going to have to stop and face this situation.

Perhaps you have read about the world's latest engineering and architectural wonder that has been constructed in St. Louis. It's a beautiful stainless steel arch that rises 640 feet above the Mississippi River. It's part of the redevelopment of downtown St. Louis, but within the shadow of that arch people live in poverty. This is all part of the Banneker District.

It's quite a contrast. St. Louis takes great pride in being "the gateway to the West." This beautiful arch is the epitome of the Chamber of Commerce's dream to draw people to St. Louis, but within the shadow of that beautiful structure there are people living in herdlike fashion in so-called "efficiency apartments"–from eight to twenty people living in three rooms. Hot water would be a novelty. A private bath would be unique. How difficult it must be to sleep, particularly the children, herded and huddled up in this fashion. Suppose one of the children is a bed-wetter. How do you expect the kids to come to school the next day–smelling like a rose? It's not likely. It's not uncommon to pick up the newspaper and read where a youngster fell out of an apartment window, or down the steps, or was burned or scalded to death because he turned over a stove or a pot of boiling water. What efforts these people make to try just to survive! When these youngsters come to school they bring problems with them that other children don't have. You must have insight into what these conditions are before you try to solve the problems.

Low Academic Achievement

The problem of low academic achievement is very great. It exists because these youngsters are not well oriented toward success in school. Their orientation is toward fighting for existence. How can these first graders know how to please the teacher? They can't. They have a different set of values. The classroom becomes an arena where frustration and defeat are inescapable. By the time these children reach third grade they are psychological dropouts. They really have not learned to read well. The work is too far over their heads. They move along in the grades because of our policies in social promotion but they're not really participants; they're not benefiting from their presence. They're just warming the seats. They only stay because the law requires it. By the time they reach the ninth, tenth, or eleventh grade, they leave at the first opportunity—they become a physical dropout.

What happens then? They'd like to work. They apply for work; they try. But what do they hear? "You don't have the educational qualifications. You don't have the training and experience so we can't employ you." One other thing has happened. They've added another year of life and now they are eligible for public assistance. If they haven't already done so, they get married; and if a child hasn't already been born, it soon will be. Then the cycle starts all over again. The irony of it is that we know what the symptoms are—we've watched the whole process from start to finish but what have we done to prevent it? The loss, measured in terms of human productivity or in terms of the dignity and worth of the individual is staggering. It reaches into every community in America. It's effects are nationwide and long-lived.

One of the basic causes of this vicious cycle is low academic achievement. The schools are in a position to attack and overcome a vulnerable link in the chain of events that leads to frustration and defeat. The elementary school must accept the challenge of providing these children with the necessary basic

[113]

skills in reading, language, and arithmetic that will allow them to profit from a first-class secondary school program.

Effecting Change—The Three Track Groupings

Two years after the Supreme Court decision desegregating the schools, our secondary schools announced a policy of grouping children in three tracks. Under this system ninth grade youngsters would be grouped on the basis of their achievement in reading, language, arithmetic and tested intelligence. We all have come to face the ugly fact in American education that youngsters in poor areas, without reference to race or religion, score anywhere from six months to four years below grade level on standardized tests. It was very clear that we had to correct this situation.

The first group of about 1,000 eighth graders that went to the high school from our district had an average intelligence score of 82.6. In Missouri, that's just a little bit above the state definition of mentally retarded. According to the prescribed standards, the majority of these children would be scheduled for track three. The curriculum in this track was designed for below average children.

In four years time we were able to raise the average I.Q. of eighth grade students from 82.6 to 95.0. We asked the Director of Tests and Measurement how he would account for this. The book says you can't change I.Q. He said that in his opinion the improvement was due to a change in the conditions affecting the student. The results of encouragement, motivation, and improved communication were impressive. We were delighted with the progress that was made. We haven't solved all our

[114]

problems. We haven't done all that can be done by any means, but we have reversed the typical situation.

I'd like to share with you the kind of morale, the team spirit that has made this kind of progress possible. The team includes the administrator, the teacher, the parent, the youngster, and even segments of the community. This morale would do credit to any winning organization or team. For example, teacher turnover in the Banneker district is very low.

This is the kind of morale that makes the difference between success or failure in the classroom and has worked to reverse the attitudes of the children. The positive attitude of the teachers and administrators toward these youngsters has in turn forced the students to have a more positive attitude toward the school, the people in it, education, learning, and achievement.

The youngsters come to school more often. When we started, the daily attendance was approximately 85 per cent of enrollment; now it is 92 per cent. One of our schools located in the poorest section of the district has a daily attendance of 94 per cent of enrollment. The children are better behaved and more interested in their work. They do better work. Behavior problems have decreased. Occasionally we have to suspend a student whose behavior cannot be tolerated but our suspension rate is very low.

The parents have been very instrumental in bringing about the improvement shown by the children. We invited them to be partners in the education of their children. We gave them a job—we involved them and their response was fantastic.

[115]

The cooperation we have received from the community agencies and business firms in our area has been wonderful. Organizations like the YWCA, Carver House, and Fellowship Center offered a real service by making their resources and facilities available to us. They provided quiet study places for those children who did not have them in their own home. The progress we have made is due to this cooperative effort and interest. The kind of change that needs to be brought about in the inner city requires the cooperation and concerted effort of everyone in the community. All the physical and human resources available must be put to the task.

The Role of the Principal

The key person in this team is the administrator. If he or she feels that achievement and success in school is dependent upon the color of the skin, the I.Q., the occupation of the father, or the number of books and magazines in the home, which we have been taught are the determinants of learning, then we aren't going anywhere. If we're not willing to abandon these notions, we might as well not begin. The same is true in terms of the teacher. If the teacher attempts to predict the maximum achievement of each child based on these external factors, we aren't going to make much progress. We started this program on a broad scale and without additional financial support because we knew that an experiment in only one school would case too much delay. We had to be courageous and make a bold move. Our approach was to start with the principals. We could see clearly what the three track program in the secondary school meant for our boys and girls. It was obvious that the opportunities for children with an 82.6 I.Q. were limited.

[116]

The first thing we did was to ask ourselves when we as principals had last been in the classroom to explain to these
youngsters what a first rate education could mean for them.
Had we ever told them how difficult it would be to get a job—to
earn a decent living? How long had it been since we last
examined the reading scores of the students in each classroom?
How much time were the students spending in the basic
reader—one month, two months, or nine months? Do we know
what's really happening in the classroom? Are the kids moving
at their own pace or at the desired pace of the teacher? We sold
our principals on the notion that they were the key to improvement. We owe whatever progress we have made to their willingness to share in the search for solutions to our problems.

This is quite a step because in St. Louis the principal has
typically thought of himself as situated up high in an ivory
tower; someone who gives a few directions and expects others
to jump. This was a crucial problem that had to be overcome.
We approached it by inviting the principals to take off their
coats, roll up their sleeves, and get in and pitch.

Our principals have come a long way. If you happen in on
one of their weekly Thursday morning meetings, you would
think it was a meeting of the Monday morning Quarterback's
Club discussing the strategy for Satuday's game. The relationship is wonderful and wholesome. We knew that we couldn't
win the battle alone—it would have to be won in the classroom.
But we have to set the tone of the relationships that would go
on between teachers and ourselves, between teachers and
teachers, between teachers and parents, and between teachers
and students. The principal can't be oblivious to this responsibility. He's got to be aware of how cliques arise and how they
operate to tear down the morale in a school faculty.

[117]

The Role of the Teacher

We asked our teachers to quit teaching by I.Q. which we described in this way: "Suppose there is a youngster, let's call her Mary, who has an average I.Q. If she hesitates a little before answering the teacher says, 'Come on Mary. You can do it. You've got to think. You know how we did it last week.' What is this teacher doing? She's pushing. She's encouraging Mary. She's motivating and she's stimulating her. She is trying to guide her and she sticks with her. But perhaps most of all, she's transferring a level of confidence that she has in Mary—and Mary understands this very well. But what happens when she calls on Charles, who has an I.Q. of 71? If he makes a grunt or two and rolls his eyes up toward the ceiling, she pats him on the shoulder saying, 'Well, that's a good try Charles. We want you here every day. We're going to water the flowers and move the pianos and you can dust the erasers every night! What is the teacher doing here? Where's the motivation? Charles can see that his teacher doesn't have any confidence in him. He wouldn't let her down for anything, because if he did, there'd be something wrong." If you analyze this situation you realize that the teacher is pretty comfortable in this kind of arrangement because she's differentiating instruction according to these numbers, and she sleeps well at night.

We asked our teachers to abandon labelling of children according to family circumstance and to reject the inclination to adopt an attitude of condescension. These are poor people and they are trapped. They are enslaved—if not in body, in mind. But they don't want pity. They want to earn our respect and we've got to find ways and means of making that possible. These people are often misunderstood. They're not stupid. They're not dumb. Some of them are living quite well on their welfare checks. Many of the 15,000 youngsters in our district are on welfare, yet we are naive enough to think they're dumb and stupid.

Ninety per cent of the teachers in our district are Negro. Most of them were born in our district. They earned a chance to improve themselves by finishing high school and going to college. When they finished college they came back to the Banneker district and got a job teaching. They got out of the slums, wear good clothes, own an automobile, and are able to live in the better part of town. This all happened because of education. It's pretty hard for the elementary teachers not to look down— not to condescend. It is even more difficult for the whites who were not in the situation in the beginning.

The cirsis in education, and I remove all qualifications, is the lack of respect that exists between the teacher and the learner. This crisis exists everywhere at every level. If the learner has the skill, he has the respect of the teacher; but if he doesn't have the skill, he isn't respected. It's universal. If the teacher is trying to teach an arithmetic problem and the youngster has no skill, the teacher unconsciously transmits this recognition of inability to the student. But this is exactly what the learner does not want. That's the problem we haven't solved in American education, period!

We asked our teachers to assign homework. There are all kinds of arguments, pro and con, about homework. But we were trying to change the attitude of students toward schools and the teachers and principals in them. Our goal was to change the attitude of the youngsters toward education, learning, and achievement from one of indifference to one of esteem and respect. Homework provided us with a wonderful vehicle to do this and we made much of it. As a matter of fact, we tied the youngsters up so that he had no alternative. We produced what is known as the Banneker district homework assignment notebook. This notebook has pages in it for assignments only. We emphasized the need to learn independent study habits and skills. We showed the youngsters a film that pointed out the various things to do, the most important of which is to remember to write down the assignment. Assigning homework was a chore for the teacher, but we felt it was very important. Every teacher in grades 4-8 was to see that there was an assignment in that notebook every day.

Then we solicited the cooperation of the parents. We asked the teachers to visit the homes. Some of the teachers and principals were apprehensive and fearful so we arranged to have a police patrol car cruising the block and one beat man walking the street while the teachers were making their calls. We released the teachers from school early so that some of their visits were made on school time. At that time our schools let out at 3:30. We agreed to start at 2:45 in the afternoon and visit until 4:00. The teachers soon realized that the police protection was unnecessary and it has been discontinued. Most of the visits are now made in the late afternoon, evening, or Sunday. It takes some skill to plan a successful program of home visitations. You have to realize that a "no" response to a request for a conference in the home may mean that the parents are too proud to have you see the condition under which they live, rather than disinterest in their children. It requires tact, empathy, and understanding.

"Mr. Achiever"

Students were asked to assist in the preparation of a script for a radio program titled "Mr. Achiever." The purpose of the program was to point out in an interesting way how well the efforts necessary to receive a good education would be rewarded. Students, teachers, and principals from our district actually played the characters in the script. Many community leaders have been Mr. Achiever guests. This program is beamed into the classroom over the PA system in each school. Mr. Achiever posters deck the halls of our schools. We miss no opportunity to stress the importance of education and to build up the children's confidence in themselves. Mr. Achiever's theme song is the old popular song, "You Can Be Better Than You Are."

Early in the spring we organize a parade with floats and marching bands to emphasize the importance of school participation. This is another opportunity to create interest and motivation in school.

The school accepts the responsibility of widening the horizons and raising the aspirations of these children. Many of them have no idea what the inside of a good theater or restaurant looks like. They've never dined out. They have no reason to learn good table manners because they have never been in a situation where these skills are required. What motivation is there to improve social behavior? The behavior that they know is all that is required in their home environment. To counteract this lack of experience each teacher arranges to take part of her students at a time to dinner in one of the city's restaurants. The students prepare for this in advance by discussing the need for being clean and well-groomed, well behaved, and mannerly, and by learning the proper way to order from a menu. New insights are developed, aspirations are raised, and meaning is given to concepts that are discussed in school.

When someone asked, "What are you trying to do? Make middle class people out of these children?" My response was, "Yes, if what we are doing will make it possible for them to earn a decent living for themselves and their families; if because of it they sense a feeling of accomplishment and self-respect; if what we are doing will make them feel they have a choice in determining their future and the future of their children; if it opens new insights into what life has to offer through responsible behavior; if what we are doing encourages participation and interest in community improvement through democratic processes then I say to you, these are the goals and objectives that guide the program in our school and to which we are strongly committed."

8

RECRUITMENT AND RETENTION OF QUALIFIED STAFF FOR CITY SCHOOLS

R. OLIVER GIBSON

THERE HAVE BEEN MANY reports of the concern expressed by prospective teachers when looking forward to the possibility of service in urban schools, particularly in inner city schools. Some report that their attitudes have been affected by parental fears or the anxieties of friends and relatives. The same people, when teachers in those schools, report unexpected satisfaction and find the experience particularly rewarding professionally.

Now let us see how we can make some sense out of what those teachers were saying. You may at times think, as I attempt to analyze what those teachers were saying, that I have gone completely off the track. At other times I may seem so abstract as to be irrelevant. But I shall try to point out the significance of my observations to the realities of the school as I have them in mind. For what I am going to suggest strikes me as very, very practical indeed, considering the nature and scope of the problem and the apparent ineffectiveness of procedures now being used to deal with it.

I shall, first of all, make a few comments about the current state of affairs in urban schools and then go on to a discussion of the factors that contribute to that state of affairs. Several

[123]

suggestions will then be given as to how the situation may be improved. Finally, a proposal which contains some implications for recruitment and retention of personnel will be presented.

Educational Affairs in Northern Cities

The processes of industrialization and migration have resulted in development of rather similar conditions in most northern cities. Included in these are such cities as Boston, New Haven, Syracuse, Rochester, Buffalo, Cleveland, Detroit, St. Louis, Chicago, and Milwaukee. The conditions common to such cities have been summarized by Havighurst:

1. A relatively low educational background of the majority of parents that is reflected in their children's school achievement.

2. A high degree of *de facto* segregation in the public schools, amounting to some 70 percent or more of Negro elementary school pupils attending schools which have a 90 percent or higher non-white enrollment.

3. A high degree of socioeconomic segregation in the public schools, with children of low-income families concentrated in certain areas of the city—usually the inner shells of the city.

4. A tendency for teachers with experience and seniority to move to the higher status schools where discipline is not much of a problem.

5. A need for flexible and varied curriculum development suited to the varying achievement levels of the various schools and of the pupils within the schools.

6. A need for high schools located where school population is increasing and also located so as to contribute to social integration of the school population.

[124]

7. A need for innovation coupled with responsible experimentation and evaluation of the results of experimentation.

8. A great deal of dissension and controversy within the public concerning the policies and practices of the school system.

Havighurst's general statements can be specified in terms of children who have never been able to see much in the way of chances in life, anger at conditions which hem in living, grand homes and cold-water flats, symphony orchestras, prostitution, special financial privilege, extortion, avant-garde groups, and inquiring study and conversation. You can fill in the picture in the schools.

What is this phenomenon that we call the "city" or the "urban center"? As we are thinking of it now it is a mental construct, a concept, or a symbol. To the Greeks it was the *polis*. The *polis* had much of the same variety of intellectual inquiry and illiteracy, poverty and opulence, special privilege and deprivation as the city of today. But the loyalty of the Greek to his city was quite a different matter than is that of the contemporary American for his city. Let us say that we symbolize the city to ourselves in ways quite different from those of the Greeks. In part, the difference relates to objective differences out there in what we call the "city." But it also seems that our habits of thinking about the city help to make the city what it is. Here we come to that very basic characteristic of man which separates him, as far as we can tell, from other animals, namely, his ability to symbolize things to himself in his own consciousness and, as a result, to make a difference in events. Cassirer has called him the *animal symbolicum*.[2] As a symbolizing animal he creates his worlds in his mind and acts out his creations in his daily life. What he thinks makes a difference. It was, I think, Chesterton who once said that in renting a room to

[125]

a man it may be more important to know how he thinks about money than to know how much he has in his pocket. It may, then, be very important to inquire about how we think about the city.

Some Human and Intellectual Aspects of the City

One of the striking aspects of how we tend to symbolize the urban center to ourselves is the frequency of use of words which suggest badness and difficulty. It probably goes back as far as Sodom and Gomorrah at least. Note our proclivity to speak of "the urban problem." In direct contrast is our concept of the wholesome, fresh, and natural countryside. Those of us who grew up in the country, if we are willing to think back, can recall much that was anything but wholesome, fresh, and natural. In between has come a symbolization of the suburb that possesses its own unreality. But the important point is that we tend to act in terms of the symbolizations, becoming nostalgic about the country, proud of the suburban status, and fearful of the evils of the city. White and White have traced some of our ideas of the city in their very suggestive book *The Intellectual Versus the City* in which they comment:

> Underlying many critiques of the American city is the ancient imperative: Follow nature. The argument built upon this imperative has been relatively simple so far as it affects the city. Man ought to follow nature, but life in the city does not follow nature; therefore, life in the city is wicked.[3]

Perhaps enough has been said to make the point that how we think about the city has much to do with what the city is, for, through acting out our conceptions of the city, we are inclined to shape it after our images. In this sense our symbolizations of the city become self-fulfilling prophecies.

[126]

Might we not just as appropriately symbolize the city in quite a different way? In many ways it would seem much more appropriate to think of the city as a place where a great variety of opportunities are available, where variety of opinion is part of life, where variety in taste and standards make possible greater scope in life, where, in sum, there is a more liberal state of affairs. It appears that new ideas and new practices are more likely to come from the city than the country. Indeed, the rural society's regard for tradition and sanctioning of strict conformity to norms is well calculated to stifle creativity. Let me then propose that it would be much more appropriate for us to symbolize the city to ourselves as the center of liberalism, creativity, and opportunity. But, unfortunately, we do not think that way. We think of the city as bad and as a problem. Like the child who, when told that he is stupid, acts on that assumption even though he may be quite bright; so also the city, after acquiring an image of problemness, comes to be treated in that light even though its cultural qualities suggest quite another image.

I am still talking about recruitment. Much of the difficulty of getting young people to entertain seriously the possibility of teaching in the city stems from the symbolization of the city that they have picked up in the family and from friends. And such problems as do occur come to be highlighted or reinforced by the habitual way of thinking. Any fundamental attack on the problems of recruitment and retention needs, it seems to me, to take into account this problem image and its self-fulfilling prophecies. It probably means that we have to examine our everyday language, encourage discussion about and contact with the city designed toward image-change. It may require new courses in colleges, early contact of prospective teachers, their friends and families, with the city schools, and a

[127]

whole variety of other approaches. City people need to overcome their problem complex and begin to think realistically about creating an opportunity image. Those qualities of the city which, hidden by the problem image, have suffered from inattention need to be highlighted and reinforced.

The limitations brought upon us by our image of the city are further confounded and complicated by other images that suffer from unreality or the deadly hand of unexamined tradition and the sanction of vested interest. We have come to think of "localism" as such a sacred concept that the city and the suburb cannot examing metropolitanism in rational terms. Some may yearn for a rational discussion concerning the location of an educational park or a hospital. However, if "Boost Buffalo" becomes a slogan that makes the rational examination of alternatives a form of community disloyalty, then the city has done something to deny its human heritage and the right of intellectually honest examination of issues.

We often further compound our misunderstandings by the ways in which we think of authority. In the name of authority administrators make regulations, the actions of government officials go unreviewed, the megalomania of officeholders bears in upon us, and reason may shrivel in its shadow. But there are hopeful signs. The public and employees are beginning to ask that statements clothed in authority have an overcoat of reason. The ombudsman, grievance procedures, and the like are coming to serve as forms of redress from capricious authority. The vestiges of feudal, personalistic privilege are being replaced by an equality that rests upon capacity to make sense. There are screams and occasional retribution emanating from those whose special privilege based upon anachronistic tradition is threatened. But the groundlines appear to be leading to the vision of a liberal society. The Negro also longs for that day.

Fundamentally important is the way that man symbolizes himself to himself. Psychology has helped us to understand how important that image is. The Coleman report documents its importance to the education of low socioeconomic children. The concept of man as essentially bad has been the justification of many aversive employment practices and the self-righteousness of central administrative officers. Our understanding of human plasticity and human capacity for response, if it is given the conditions under which it can flourish, seems to justify an almost unbounded confidence in human capacity for development.

Finally, what is our image of education? Conventionally we have pictured it to ourselves as "transmission of culture." Defined in that sense, education becomes an essentially conservative and maintaining force in society. As Coleman suggests, it seems appropriate to think of education as a self-reproducing system.[4] But today the great need is not to pass on the evils of yesterday and its prejudices. The need is for a change, a rebirth. It may be that we need to think of education as a self-renewing system—a system under which culture gets reviewed, refreshed, and revitalized. If so, then we can see the school as a force for social renewal. That, it seems to me, is precisely what the problem of integration is demanding of the schools.

The point is that much of what we call problems today stem in large part from how we think about ourselves and our condition. It all leads very naturally to asking about how we can think in some useful fashion about the school as an institution and what it means for recruitment and retention.

[129]

Creating an Image of the School

It seems useful to me to think of the school as a social system. By that I mean a number of positions related together into a structural whole. The criteria for inclusion in the system provide a boundary separating it from its environment. The degree of permeability of the boundary determines how open or closed the system is. Closed systems tend to have impermeable boundaries, are defensive toward the environment, have strict rules and regulations, and tend toward sameness of structure which locks in energy thus increasing entropy.

Open systems have the opposite characteristics; high boundary permeability, accepting toward the environment, flexible rules and regulations, and differentiation of structure that releases energy thus decreasing entropy.

Ultimately the closed system is in danger of self-destruction through rigidity and isolation. The open system is ultimately in danger of being absorbed by its environment. In between is the sort of system which possesses sufficient openness to grow and adapt but still retain its identity. This we can call a *viable* system.

The school seems to me to be a system whose characteristics get to be determined in important ways by certain boundary questions. Systems such as schools, hospitals, prisons, and the services, need to be very clear about when their clients or members are part of the system and when they are in the environment. For the school it has to do with when the child is in the home and when the school is *in loco parentis.* Various court cases have sought to determine the boundary point. The rituals of boundary crossing tend to be very clear in both time and

[130]

place, e.g., registration for school or admission to a hospital. Thus the boundary tends to have low permeability and the system takes on some of the characteristics of a closed system. In this respect the school could be expected to have the characteristics, to a degree, of the closed system, reacting rather defensively toward the community, emphasizing conformity to rules and regulations, and developing uniformity of structure which restricts initiative and participation. It is with a good deal of regret that I confess that my logic seems to bring me to something only too like the schools out there in reality. But there are also schools scattered along the continuum from closedness toward openness. My impression is that there is a clustering toward the closed end. There are studies which give credence to this position.

This conclusion brings us to a very important matter. The research concerning teachers and their work suggests that teachers, like workers in some other fields, derive their satisfactions primarily from their work and their dissatisfactions largely from the environing systems.[5] Teachers like to do meaningful work and to handle it to their own satisfaction with minimal environing constraint. A closed system tends to restrict work discretion and to increase system constraint. Under such circunstances one could expect that there would be considerable dissatisfaction with work and aggression directed toward the central office. This problem is becoming aggravated these days. The level of professional competence of teachers is either rising or they think it is, or both. In either case teachers are coming to want to exercise more control over the center of satisfaction, their work. Thus they are pressing for a more open system. But a closed system, by definition, has a rather low capacity for response. It strikes me that all this has something to do with a lot of the turbulence that is going on in schools these days. It appears quite safe to predict that either the turbulence will increase or the schools will take on more open characteristics.

Let me illustrate with one area of teacher concern—class size. Teachers say they want small classes. It is my impression, supported in the literature, that they want to do a good piece of work and they do not mind having a fairly large class so long as it does not get in the way of doing a good job. However, when the system sets up the class situation in such a way as to make good work performance more difficult, they become more dissatisfied. When problem children are placed in the classroom and they make it difficult for the learning process to take place the teacher becomes unhappy. Again, it is my impression that the teacher does not mind having a class the size that other teachers have so long as her work is not handicapped by problem cases that should have specialized attention.

It strikes me that urban schools are rather susceptible to taking on the characteristics of the closed system. Havighurst pointed out, as quoted above, that the northern urban school tends to be subject to community criticism and pressure. We have also noted some of the problems that arise from customary ways of thinking about the city, authority, and the school. It may very well be that these all conspire to make the urban system, in some cases at least, rather closed. The apparent defensiveness and structural rigidity in some city systems leads me to surmise that there is something to my speculations.

Havighurst also has alluded to what he calls the "four-walled" school and the "community" school, arguing that the urban school, if it is to cope with its contemporary challenge, needs to move from its four-walled status toward that of a community school. In terms of the present formulation, the urban school needs to become less closed and more open. There is, by definition, a problem in all this. For, if the school becomes too open toward the community, it may lose its renewal capacity. The school that possesses a functional degree of openness would then be a viable school. It would be open enough to respond to the human needs of the community and to be supportive of the human needs of its teachers. Let us call such a viable school, perhaps for want of a better term, a *humanistic* school. It is my hunch that, were it possible to develop such a school together with a more constructive image of the city, urban schools would find the tasks of recruitment and retention much less pressing.

You may now feel rather disenchanted that you have been brought to this rather utopian abstraction that bears little practical relevance to what actually occurs in the schools. However, let us see what we might do about setting up a rationale and some practices, by focusing upon work relationships and how they might be set up in a satisfying manner. In the following proposal a policy position of the board will first be suggested and a plan will then be outlined.

A Proposal for Work Organization to Enhance Recruitment and Retention

A proposed policy statement of the board. It is our intent that the schools of our city will serve to make possible for all people, young and old, life that is good in all its ways. To this end we want to share in all that man has come to know and appreciate. We want to go on to fresh insights into what is true and what is good. Particularly, we are concerned about racial and economic deprivation in our midst. When affairs are so arranged, either by circumstance or design, that the very young are caught in the grasp of deprivation and isolation we cannot escape the likelihood that the situation ". . . . may affect their hearts and minds in a way unlikely every to be undone."[6] We see as a primary and urgent need the establishment and maintenance of the conditions in the schools that open up for all young people meaningful life chances and that speed them on their way to acceptance and accomplishment.

The conditions which give rise to concern have been with us for some time and have taken root deeply in the customs and motivations of society. When a condition so pervasive in our city bears in upon the schools, the schools cannot hope to help solve the problem, except in commitment and action shared with the community. In part because the condition has been with us for a long time, the urgency of that shared commitment and action is today acute. It appears to us that particularly relevant is a genuine shared commitment with all groups who can make common cause with us for quality integrated education for all. In that cooperative community endeavor we foresee the possibility of productive action with community groups, both formal and voluntary, with the several branches of city government, with the organizations of teachers and other staff members, and with the several state and federal agencies, both public and private. In sum, we see an obligation to undertake a comprehensive educational program aimed at reversing a pervasive social condition that has become deeply rooted in our society.

We do not know that we have yet seen the ways by which the changes may best be effected. We are, however, confident that we should make the best use possible of what we already know and, through sincere cooperative effort, seek educational pathways to a better society.

We would argue that such aspirations are now urgently called for. And it is our expectation that the staff of the public schools will share those aspirations, both in their work and through their associations, to the end that they may be converted into social realities.

Recruitment and retention policies are intended to identify, bring to our schools, and retain the teachers who can make education a lively part of urban living. These policies should reflect the scope and diversity of our social and intellectual life. We expect, therefore, that our administrators and teachers will develop specific plans for the ways in which they can help the community to accomplish the kind of education we desire. Those plans will include the ways in which they propose to bring to the schools the staff that is needed. We are not at all concerned whether the staff is certified or not; we do, however, expect that the administrators and teachers will be able to show how their judgments relate to the standards of their several professional groups and that they will from time to time provide an assessment of how the results of their plans and activities relate to our educational aspirations. We hope, however, that critical examination will be a continuing activity which the staff and the community will undertake seriously and vigorously. In this sense we look forward to a school program which demonstrates to all a model of an intellectually vigorous and self-examined life.

A proposal for instructional staff grouping. We turn now to a proposal which we can assume has been formulated by the administration and the staff and is advanced as a reasonable approach to the kind of education indicated above as desired by the board. The plan rests upon what we know about how people behave socially, upon the realities of the manpower resources available, and certain practical needs of running the schools. It will be argued on those grounds that the traditional staffing practices be replaced by a program of instructional staff grouping. Since its potential has much to offer for recruitment and retention in inner city schools, the proposal is that it be initiated in those schools, with primary emphasis upon the elementary schools.

The recommended program is seen as promoting desirable education as well as providing a number of operational advantages.[7] There is a very substantial and growing body of knowledge that points up the social nature of people and the implications for how work can be organized. These findings raise questions about the rather isolating effect upon the teacher of the self-contained classroom limiting, as it seems to do, the sharing of experience, skill, professional insight, and instructional tasks. The sort of sharing through groups just suggested opens the way to the instructional gains that can come from teachers working at the tasks that they can do best. It opens the way to continuing and functional sharing of the insight of more experienced teachers with those who are entering, thinking of entering, or helping with instruction. Such a group, insofar as it is socially and professionally supportive of the members of the group, can be helpful to the individual in finding a personal and professional identity. In sum, the proposed program of teaching groups is seen as a social soil in which meaningful personal and professional growth can take place.

Perhaps even more compelling is the argument that arises from the need for efficient and effective use of limited manpower resources of highly competent professionals. There is an escalating demand for such persons in all sectors of our society.

While at the turn of the century about 4 per cent of the labor force was in the professional-technical sector, by mid-century it had doubled to about 8 per cent and another doubling to about 16 per cent is expected by about 1975. At the same time teachers are becoming a smaller portion of the professional-technical sector. In the midst of the growing competition for professional personnel, it seems reasonable to question whether it is feasible or desirable to continue to work on the assumption of being able to obtain one outstanding teacher for every fifteen to thirty or thirty-five pupils in the schools. Indeed, unless schools can maintain a really competitive status not only in terms of economic remuneration but also in terms of professional rewards for teaching, it would seem almost likely that the general level of quality in the teaching force will decline. An instructional group program need not reduce the ratio of regularly certified teachers to pupils and, in the program recommended here, it does not. Indeed, it will be argued that the program will serve to retard or even reverse the possible decline in quality.

There is an urgent need for personnel policies and programs that are calculated to cope with the above realities. One element of such a program would seem to be an emphasis upon at least a core staff of highly competent teachers in each school. Just what would be the critical ratio to the whole staff is a matter for further study. The members of the core staff of a particular school provide the personnel who can serve as leaders in the recommended instructional groups. In so doing they have the opportunity to affect daily the performance of other members of the staff and to counteract the potential negative effects of escalating competition already mentioned. In general, then, it is argued that instructional grouping provides one realistic approach (not in itself sufficient) by which schools can cope with escalating competition for competent professional personnel.

The advantages in terms of accomplishment resulting from division of labor have been formulated by different economists. Instructional tasks may be divided in a number of ways. Instructional content, probably the most frequently considered, is but one basis. Level of complexity of skill, interest, and professional maturity are some other bases. More than one basis might be combined in creating a division of labor within a group and the basis might shift from time to time. Thus, the group with its division of labor opens up possibilities of more effective and flexible use and development of the varied talents of the staff.

Implementation of a program of organizing instruction in small teaching groups is bound to run into a number of difficulties. In many ways practices and facilities have been developed on assumptions of one teacher and a number of pupils. Many teachers and administrators may be eminently recalcitrant to the changes that new times make necessary. Facilities very frequently do not lend themselves to instruction by teaching groups. A combination of humane personnel relationships, professional concern, and imaginative adaptation can do much to overcome the limitations of custom and structure.

The alternative to meaningful reorganization of the work of teaching by remaining in the grip of custom and facilities offers a bleak prospect with the all too great likelihood of a degeneration of the quality of instruction in schools.

On the other hand, implementation of the program recommended here opens the way to a number of operational advantages. The teaching group is calculated to enhance social and work identification or involvement. There is considerable evidence to suggest that such a development is likely to be associated with reduction in frequency of absence and turnover in the staff. It is also likely to be associated with greater involvement in instructional tasks. Also, because the group has a degree of flexibility through its ability to distribute tasks among its members, it can adapt to emergencies and absences of its members in ways individual teachers cannot. Thus, the flexibility of teaching groups provides a way of coping with the many agonizing problems of the occasional substitute affecting, in all probability, the total pattern of substitute service.

Perhaps the greatest operational advantage of the teaching group is the fact that in-service preparation is functionally built into day-by-day work. There is much evidence to suggest that this approach to in-service work is more likely to change behavior than are lectures, workshops on synthetic problems, and conferences. It has already been suggested that the in-service aspect of the instructional work group may be of critical importance for the upgrading or even the maintenance of reasonable standards of staff quality.

The group also opens up possibilities for recruitment as well as for upgrading skills. There are already reports of experience in which persons serving in such roles as aides have developed identification with teaching, and have set about to prepare for such a career. It is here that the instructional work group approach is particularly relevant for inner city schools. It makes possible utilization of a number of persons not now in the instructional force, including mothers of grown families and such ethnic groups as Negroes, Puerto Ricans, and Mexicans. As part of the preparation of student teachers, if the identification idea is at all correct, practice in such a group can lead to greater depth of insight into the problems and possibilities of the inner city school and to interest in service in those schools.

Furthermore, the instructional group can provide the supportive climate necessary for the early development of professional self-confidence. Such social support can be of critical importance, particularly in inner city schools, in building the interest, insight, and confidence that may lead to continued service in these schools. While this support can prove valuable to teachers at all stages of their development, it is probably most pertinent to the young teacher haunted by the fears and uncertainties prevalent in our ways of thinking about the inner city.

The ways in which flexible instructional work groups can be developed are, no doubt, many depending upon the interests, facilities, and needs of particular schools. Research and exper-ience to date do not provide a firm basis for any one pattern for groups. At the risk of seeming to advocate a particular pattern, one possibility is now proposed. It might prove sensible in some situations to think in terms of a group of at least seven mem-bers, perhaps more typically a group of ten. Such a group might consist of one core-staff teacher who serves as leader, three regular less experienced teachers, a beginning teacher, two practice teachers or interns, and three aides. Let us assume that one such group is assigned for each 150 pupils. Then in a school of 1,500 pupils there would be a core-staff of ten particularly able teachers, thirty regular less experienced teachers, ten beginning teachers, twenty practice teachers or interns, and thirty aides, including such persons as members of the teacher corps. In accordance with this policy, instructional staff quotas can be developed by the central staff and they can be allocated by districts or areas of the city with specific assignments made by district or area administrators and principals. Principals should be encouraged to test out and assess the feasibility of various forms of instructional groups.

These are some glimmerings of what the proposed humanistic school might be like. You might try your hand at creating an image of a viable urban school system calculated to help in the recruitment and retention of teachers.

It was first argued that much of our difficulty regarding the city stems from a negative image of the city. The influence of a negative city image is increased by traditional ways of thinking about such matters as authority, people, and education. There is a real need for image change.

Social systems were seen as having different degrees of openness or closedness along a distribution from one to the other. Schools seem to be located toward the closed end of the distribution. The urban situation needs schools that are more open. Upon this basis the humanistic school has been proposed as a viable system for these times.

Stemming from the above considerations a proposed statement of policy for an urban school board has been formulated and a related staffing program has been advanced. The staffing program, aimed directly at improved recruitment and retention, emphasizes structuring the staff in work groups that can help to attract and retain staff members. The program seems to make social, psychological, economic, and organizational sense. In detail the proposed might be applied in many different ways by local school staffs.

NOTES

1. Robert J. Havighurst, "Chicago's Educational Needs–1966," in *Educating an Urban Population,* Marilyn Gittell (ed.) (Beverly Hills, California: Sage Publications, Inc., 1967), pp. 37-38.

2. Ernst Cassirer, *An Essay on Man* ([orig. pub. 1944], Garden City, N.Y.: Anchor Books, Doubleday & Co., Inc., 1953), p. 44.

3. Morton White and Lucia White, *The Intellectual Versus the City* (Cambridge, Mass.: Harvard University Press and The M.I.T. Press, 1967), p. 233.

4. James S. Coleman *et al., Equality of Educational Opportunity* (Washington, D.C.: U.S. Government Printing Office, 1966), p. 310.

5. I am indebted here to graduate students Charles F. Adams and Allan Freedman who have provided helpful suggestions.

6. *Brown* v. *Board of Education,* 1954.

7. These ideas were developed in discussions with members of the central office of the Chicago Public Schools and their contributions are here acknowledged.

9

THE URBAN SCHOOL SYSTEM OF TOMORROW

FRANK J. DRESSLER

ANY SPECULATION ON the future of urban school systems must, of necessity, start with today's accomplishments, limitations, and problems. When one undertakes the task of cataloguing these factors, it becomes apparent that it is not possible to consider all of them within the scope of this paper. Consequently, it is necessary to make choices and to devote attention to those factors which seem, if not more critical, at least basic to the future task of providing quality education for all the children of the urban center. As a result of this choice-making the problem of the most desirable pattern of grade organization for the urban school and the question of the location and size of schools in an urban center will not be considered. Consideration to the 4-4-4 plan of school organization, the education park concept and the busing of pupils are critical educational, social, and political issues in our urban centers. But the sense of urgency that surrounds them is an aspect of the great social revolution through which the United States is now passing. Omission of these factors is not an attempt to ignore the importance of racial integration in the schools. However, the present situation is so fluid, so mixed with changing and conflicting values and emotions, that one hesitates to predict the outcome. The remarks which follow are intended instead to draw attention to other basic issues related to the quality education—quality education which will operate for the benefit of all children in all patterns of grade and school organization.

[143]

Organizing Future Schools

The urban school of tomorrow, if it is to meet the needs of urban children with a wide range of differences in cultural, economic and social background, ability and interest in school, must be organized on a different basis than are the schools of today. Its goals must be the continuous development of understanding of knowledge to the best of the child's and the school's ability, the development of the skills of problem-solving, and the growth of personal and social maturity. Its organization must provide for the continuous adjustment of the curriculum to the factors of change in our society. Providing for individual differences in the ability and growth of children, and for adaptation to change, have long been objectives expounded by educators. But everyone closely connected with city schools, in fact with most schools, knows that the concern for these objectives is frequently more verbal than actual.

The basic device used to adapt instruction to individual differences today has been the introduction of various practices of grouping based on assumed differences in levels of ability and achievement. These procedures have proven to be ineffective for several reasons: First, the degree of our knowledge of variations in human ability and growth and our means of measuring these factors is not sufficient to warrant treating children in this way. Sceond, our feeble attempts at curriculum revision to meet assumed levels of ability are entirely valid justification.

We do not have valid criteria on which to base decisions as to which body of content is more appropriate for a slow learner than for a fast learner. Nor do we know with any degree of certainty what aspects of the curriculum are more easily learned

[144]

by "slow learners." By and large, we have watered down the traditional content of most subjects and the examinations to the point where the assumed slow learner can pass, hoping that in the process he has gained something useful. Many children do not believe that what they are gaining in school is valuable, and they cast their negative vote by dropping out or by remaining in school in body—but not in mind.

The basic devices used to adapt schools to change today are to alter the organizational structure and to alter the curriculum. Both of these approaches have merit if it can be shown that the changes will bring about improvement in meeting the needs of children. All too often this is not the case. Changes in grade organization frequently are administrative changes made to meet space needs, community pressures, and state mandates. The assumed educational values are rationalized later.

Curriculums are modified for much the same reason. Local group pressures require the introduction or modification of certain subjects or areas of content. Regional accrediting agencies, the college board of examinations, the state education department, the state legislature, self-appointed foundations or groups of content specialists prepare and/or dictate the subjects to be taught and the material to be studied in each subject. These efforts at change almost universally reflect adult concepts—concepts frequently based upon the ignorance of knowing nothing or of knowing too much about a specific area. Seldom are they related to the developmental pattern of individual children nor are they designed to help the child to develop problem-solving skills, or to grow in personal and social maturity; rather, they seek to impose on children a pattern of information that is often useless and sterile, and whose primary value is to help him pass the final examinations.

[145]

Individualizing Instruction

The urban school of tomorrow must escape from much that is common practice in education today. Goals and objectives must be re-evaluated. If the purpose of education is to provide for maximum understanding of knowledge, to develop skills in problem-solving, and to encourage personal and social maturity, then the curriculum, methods of instruction, use of instructional tools, grade placement patterns, evaluation procedures, and building facilities will have to be altered since these factors are all interrelated. Alteration of these aspects will be useless, however, unless they are accompanied by changes affecting the preparation and work realtionships of the professional staff.

This sounds like a very formidable set of changes, and indeed it is. But the situation is not hopeless. In an educational system organized for change, the ultimate goal is never reached. What is important is movement in the right direction—the direction of teaching individuals not groups.

The first requirement for individualizing instruction is to know the achievement level of each child at all times. Instruction must start where the child is and not where the teacher thinks he ought to be. Teacher evaluation of progress is very effective when the teacher has the opportunity to get to know the child and his developmental problems. From time to time teacher judgment should be checked against standardized tests.

The next requirement is to custom-tailor a curriculum to provide for the continuous educational growth of each child. This may sound utopian, but nothing less will do if we are to provide for the maximum development of each child. Needless to say, the adaptation of the curriculum to the child will lead to new concepts and practices about grading, promotion, and grade placement. But these new concepts will not be as far removed from actual practice in the schools as we might first assume. We still talk of grade achievement standards, but in reality they have become quite flexible. What is really new is that the flexibility will be based upon rational planning and not upon chance and/or necessity.

In the primary years, the curriculum and instructional emphasis will continue to be placed upon the communication skills related to reading and arithmetic. These subjects are essential, since they deal with the organized patterns of symbols that open doors to the stored knowledge of the world.

In the intermediate years, the development of the communication skills must be continued. However, when we look at the rest of the educational program, we find that careful evaluation and rethinking is needed. Certainly science, social studies, and literature are keys to important areas of life. But so are health education, child growth and development, sex education, human relations, racial relations, economics, government, international relations and an understanding of the world of work which goes far beyond the concept of community helpers.

Specialized curriculum workers should be continuously involved with the community, the teachers, and the pupils to determine the individual needs of each child and how they can best be met in the school. Curriculum development should be approached as a flexible, individual problem. Perfect answers for all time need not be sought, since change is anticipated and accepted. The urban school should be committed to the experimental approach. An ongoing program of evaluation must be built into the system. There should be no hesitancy to discard that which is ineffective in satisfying the objectives of the school.

At the secondary level the need for emphasis upon the skills of communication continues on a more mature level. The new concepts previously proposed for the intermediate curriculums designed to help the child better understand himself and his role in society, must be expanded. Additional concepts from psychology, sociology, economics, and other areas of learning must find their way into the curriculum along with history, algebra, chemistry, and the other traditional areas.

Special effort should be made in the school to help the child prepare for the world of work. The nature of most jobs has become more complicated and more specialized; the opportunities of the child to learn about types of jobs, what they are, and what they require of him, are limited. In many cases, the child has only a vague idea of what his father does to earn a living. His experiences in growing up have not prepared him for realistic decision-making in this area. The urban school of tomorrow must do much more to help the child make a wise choice. This preparation must start in the early grades and the emphasis must be greatly increased during the early secondary years. Teachers and guidance counselors should work as a team to help each child make a wise occupational choice. As the child's occupational interests begin to develop and crystallize, provision should be made for visits to places of employment and other experiences which will help him identify areas for further study.

The later secondary years have become a period of specialization in preparation for work for many children. This preparation may be very specific, as in the case of a boy learning to be a machinist, or it may be open-ended, as in the case of the person taking college entrance in the expectation this will open the door to further educational opportunities. In any case, a choice has to be made and this usually occurs during the eighth or ninth grades.

Hopefully, in time, children will not be forced to make an occupational choice before the end of their secondary education program. At such time all specialized education will be conducted at the post high school level. Unfortunately, however, such a change will have to wait until the general educators have developed curriculums and methods which are more meaningful and more attractive to many of the young persons in the schools.

The greatest single curriculum problem confronting the urban school of tomorrow is the necessity to identify and develop a useful pattern of education for those young persons who do not have the ability or the interest and motivation to want to prepare for college entrance or for the skilled vocational trades. This group finds much of present day general education meaningless to them. It is often completely unrelated to their lives and their interests and appears to lack direction and usefulness. This group is large and in most instances, it is growing. It is in this group that the largest number of dropouts occur, and it is also in this group that many discipline problems occur. Certainly such a pattern will contain elements of the traditional academic program. Some of the new concepts previously proposed, concepts which relate more specifically to the child and his current needs, will prove to be a significant part of the pattern as will general occupational training around clusters of related work activities. This is not a proposal for a diluted vocational program, but rather a plea for the development of a new type of occupational education which will prepare the youth for entry into a variety of positions within a broad occupational area.

Changes in Methodology

If the urban school of tomorrow is to be organized around the individual and his needs, the curriculum is not the only part of the program in need of revision; equally important are changes in methodology. Teaching procedures which are designed primarily for work with groups will have to be modified to include a great deal of individual or small group instruction. Learning experiences will have to be related to the needs of each child at his stage of development rather than to the assumed level of accomplishment indicated by the grade or the curriculum. More emphasis will need to be placed upon the continuous evaluation of progress. Alternate methods will have to be tried if the first method fails. Above all, methods will need to be developed that place great emphasis upon the development of problem-solving skills. Children should learn the sources of information, how to evaluate and organize knowledge, and how to use knowledge to reach conclusions and to develop patterns of action. Such procedures will be infinitely more valuable to the child than the ability to recall numerous facts. In addition, if the development of personal and social maturity is accepted as a goal of education, the child must be allowed to grow. He must be given opportunities for self-direction and for valid group participation. The iron hand and the iron will of the teacher must become more gentle, for the skills of self-direction and self-discipline do not flourish in a dictatorship, even a benevolent one.

Above all, methodology must be determined by the critical needs of the child. If the child's failure in reading is caused by poor eyesight, the methodology is obvious—get him to an eye doctor. If his failure is caused by lack of concept-forming experiences and he is unable to understand the meaning of word symbols, the methodology again is obvious—provide him with the needed experiences.

I do not propose to guess at an optimum class size or teacher-pupil ratio. This will vary depending upon the ability and the needs of the children. What is important is that each child be engaged in useful activity that will contribute to his educational growth. The dull hours of involvement with busy work, the physical and intellectual repression of much class procedure, must come to an end.

Obviously, these suggestions will require the employment of more teachers, teacher assistants, librarians, more specialists of every category. But this is the price of quality education. If our experiences with Head Start (Early Push) programs and compensatory education, as provided under Title I of the E.S.E.A. have told us anything, it is that if you assign greater resources to a task, you can expect to gain greater results.

The new methodology will require an increased use of a wider variety of instructional materials or tools. Books will still be used. In fact, we still need lots of books—books organized in carefully worked out developed stages, and books with no set pattern, except that they deal with a wide range of ideas and events which are of interest to young people. We will need books with varying levels of reading difficulty and books with varying levels of interest to children.

We will not be able to limit our instructional tools to books and related printed materials. Man has always organized, recorded, and sought to perpetuate his knowledge by the use of the latest technology available. The cave man drew his pictures on the cave wall, since this was the only method available to him. When printing was developed, knowledge and education made a great leap forward. It became easier to organize, record, and perpetuate knowledge.

The schools are still operating primarily in the age of books, although technology has passed beyond this point and has provided many other useful means of communicating ideas. The optical projector has been available for years, but sees limited use in classrooms. Radio and TV, two of the most effective devices for communicating ideas and building values in the adult world, have still to come into their own as educational tools in schools. Record players and other recording devices are in the same category. Even more sophisticated electronic tools like teaching machines, talking typewriters, and computers are being developed and will be available for use in the classroom.

These innovations have great potential for aiding the teacher, for improving instruction, and above all, individualizing instruction. The urban school of tomorrow will have to learn how to utilize these machines as aids to instruction.

It follows that school buildings and related facilities will need to be modified to provide for new teaching methods and instructional tools. The familiar square classroom will have to be replaced with rooms of varying sizes adaptable to flexible uses. Experimental programs have already established patterns of this type of school facility. The task for the urban school is to actually create such facilities and to put them to use.

The Modern Teacher

Individualization of instruction—new curriculum— flexibility—continuous change—use of new instructional devices— how is the teacher going to adapt to all this? We know that one of the reasons for the lag in educational innovation today, is the insecurity felt by many teachers in the face of new knowledge, methods, and tools. Unless some way can be found to help the teacher and to prepare him for the changing patterns in education, very little that has been proposed will happen. The preparation of the teacher is the key, for the action occurs when the teacher meets the student in the schoolroom.

One great weakness of education today is our reliance upon the teacher to keep himself professionally competent. After five years of college the teacher is expected to be prepared for a career spanning thirty or forty years. All factors point to the need for continuous retraining of the teacher in knowledge, skills, attitudes, and values.

How are we to acquire this modern teacher? Part of the responsibility rests with the teacher preparation programs of the colleges and universities to modify their programs toward greater reality. Part of the responsibility rests, as now, with the teacher and his professional interest and desire for growth.

But these factors are not enough. The urban school system must assume greater responsibility for the retraining and updating of its professional staff. The present practice of granting extra salary for extra college credits helps, but it is not adequate. Just as the army and industry recognize the cost of retraining personnel as part of their operating costs, so must the school system.

[153]

Teachers should be periodically evaluated to determine the need for additional training. Those who are found lacking in knowledge or methodology should be assigned to a college program or to an advanced school maintained by the school system and taught both by college and public school personnel. This assignment would be the regular and full assignment of the teacher for the required period of time and at no reduction in salary.

In addition to these more extensive renewal classes, the urban school should conduct a continuous series of short in-service programs for teachers. These would be designed to give insight into some specific problem or to develop skill in the use of some specific procedures. These courses should be conducted during regular school hours or after hours in which case teachers would receive additional compensation for attending.

All that has been said about the limitations and needs of teachers also applies to administrators. Being promoted from the classroom to the office does not usually make essential differences in a person. The nonchalant are still nonchalant, the eager are still eager—what has changed is the role in the educational process that the person is expected to assume. Each has its particular pressures, responsibilities, and limitations. The title of principal, supervisor, director, or superintendent confers no special talent or ability, although it may give the person an opportunity to see and appreciate additional aspects of the total educational structure. Administrators need in-service education and updating the same as do teachers, and the urban school system of the future should provide the opportunities.

No effort will be made to promulgate a more perfect administrative and/or supervisory setup than that which exists in urban schools today. There appears to be no general pattern or procedure. Administrative structures are historical and appear to have developed in relation to need, to community pressures, and to the impact of personnel. However, as the instructional program is individualized, the teaching staff is enlarged, and new and complicated instructional tools are introduced, there will be a need for additional and more specialized administrators and supervisors. The use of the word supervisor may not express the proper connotation. What is needed now and will be needed in the future are skilled, competent, and emotionally mature persons whose primary job will be to help teachers adjust to the many problems with which they will be confronted.

Effective Communication

The last proposal for improvement in the urban school of tomorrow relates to a serious problem in today's schools—the problem of communication between the various parts of the total school structure. Communication is needed from the top to all echelons below and from them back to the top. Many cross-patterns of communication also are needed—teachers to teachers, principals to principals, etc. Unless there is communication, change as proposed herein is not possible. All personnel must know the objectives of the school and why these objectives have been selected—all personnel must have a commitment to achieve these objectives. Knowledge and commitment have their roots in the processes of communication.

The effectiveness of communication is usually assumed to be a function of size. There is no evidence that size is more important than people, but assuming the same personnel, size does increase the difficulty of the problem.

All school systems develop structures and procedures for communication. These include such well-known institutions as: the faculty meeting after school, the superintendent's staff meetings, meetings of principals, and other discrete groups, committee involvement in curriculum work, textbook selection, preparation of tests, and advisory committees of various types. All of these devices serve a useful purpose, but do not solve the basic problem.

Too many meetings and committees are devoted to routine administrative functions and become characterized as techniques for direction-giving rather than as means for communication. Another problem is that each member of the school team—the teacher, the principal, the supervisor, the superintendent—is primarily interested in his own function. They perceive themselves in a special role and frequently they do not listen, even when they talk to one another.

The urban school of tomorrow will have to create a new structure for communication. This should consist of an organized series of in-service meetings involving all teachers and dealing with the specific administrative and teaching problems that exist in the school system. These in-service sessions should deal with such topics as the importance of community pressures upon educational policy and curriculum, the relation of the board of education to the political structure of the community and to the staff, the financial problems confronting the schools and the city, problems of recruitment and the staffing of schools, practices used in teacher evaluation, reasons for curriculum change, problems of discipline, and the relation of administrative practices to teacher methodology.

Obviously, such a proposal will be costly in staff, in time, and in dollars but there are no bargain rates for quality education, and teacher-administration communication is a part of the cost of securing quality education.

In an urban school system, with many children of widely varying abilities, backgrounds, and interests quality education can be achieved only by a high degree of individualization of instruction. Attention to individual differences is not a new idea—but effective implementation of this concept in a school system is.

This is not a panacea that will solve all educational problems. There are many aspects which have been left uncovered and unaswered. But if the urban school of tomorrow is to flourish and be effective, it must operate upon the concepts of individual differences and of continuous change.

Part IV

THE ORGANIZATION

AND

ADMINISTRATION

OF URBAN SCHOOLS

10

COMMUNICATION PROBLEMS IN LARGE ORGANIZATIONS

WARREN G. BENNIS

I'D LIKE TO DISCUSS a matter which concerns human organizations. More specifically, I's like to talk about the problems people face in organizations, particularly in a world which is undergoing rapid and turbulent change, and how these problems affect communication. The problem of communication generally is a function of some of the main problems affecting large social systems and organizations. I want to speak broadly and I want to try to pinpoint certain problems that I believe exist in school systems.

The study of human organizations is a relatively new field. A group that called itself "Organizational Studies" was organized at MIT in 1959. Harvard Business School started its program in the early 1960s. It's a very new field in the sense that for the first time scholars are systematically giving attention to how people relate to each other in organizations in an attempt to understand how to develop organizational systems where people can be more creative and productive. Very little is known about what goes on in organizations even though man has been living in organizations for a long period of time. Only recently have we begun turning our attention to them. The field now appears to be moving away from looking only at *people* within these organizations to looking at the *culture* of the organization and the organizational system. In other words, there is a movement away from personnel psychology to organizational psychology.

Bringing About Change in Organizations

The study of the culture of an organization requires the definition of organizational norms. It isn't enough to just change a person, to remove a boss from an organization or to bring somebody else in to bring about change in an organization. The problems of changing organizations are far more profound and deal with the whole cultural matrix, the whole normative system. The customs of the organization must be changed. Some years ago International Harvester sent a number of their foremen to a human relations training course in an attempt to develop better techniques of administration. At the end of the three-month period it was determined that most of the people did change along the dimensions that were established for the course. However, the fade-out effect of the training was enormous when they returned to their work. As a matter of fact, certain people regressed below what they were before they went to the training school because they were so upset at the kind of contradictoriness between what they learned in the training program and what actually existed in the organization. Unless the organization reinforces the learner, sending individuals away for a residential period of time in a training program simply doesn't work. It takes more than a few new ideas to change a system. There is a far more profound set of things that need to be done.

At this point I should like to make an evolutionary hypothesis. The hypothesis is this: every age develops an organizational form appropriate to its genius. Every age develops new forms of organization that are most appropriate to the needs and tasks of the time. The basic point here is that the bureaucratic structure, usually talked about with some disdain by government and lay people as being hierarchal, pyramidal, imbedded, rigid, endowed

[162]

with concentrated power, and specialization of function with rules that are very clearly defined, has been a very useful organization for harnessing the muscle power needed for the tasks of the nineteenth century. However, the hierarchal form of organization really isn't appropriate for the kinds of tasks that we're facing today. The reason we're having communication problems in organizations today is because the kind of organization most of us are working with is this form of a pyramid with power concentrated at the top and with orders percolating down. This kind of an organization just isn't up to the sorts of tasks, demands, and people that we have today. The two are out of joint with each other; consequently, different forms of organization are being developed.

The key word of these organizations of the future is temporary. They will be adaptive, rapidly changing, temporary systems which will consist of task forces organized around problems to be solved by groups of relative strangers with diverse professional backgrounds and skills. The groups will be arranged on an organic rather than a mechanical model, meaning they will evolve in response to a problem rather than to preset programmed expectations. People will be evaluated not vertically according to rank and status, but flexibly according to competence. Organizational charts will consist of project groups rather than stratified function groups.

Why is the pyramidal form of organizational bureaucracy inadequate? There are four main reasons which should be pointed out, each of which is a key feature of our society. First of all, bureaucracy was developed at a time when most people in the world thought that rapid change would no longer occur. The development of most bureaucratic organizations and certainly the theoretical writings came out around the turn of

[163]

the century. Max Weber, the German sociologist was really the first student of bureaucracy and wrote his theory of bureaucracy around 1910. During those Victorian times most people felt that significant changes and inventions had already been made. As a matter of fact, the Royal Patent Office around the turn of the century in England, was thinking of closing because they thought most significant inventions had already been made. In fact, there was talk in our Congress about the same period of time, suggesting that the U.S. Patent Office be closed. While it's now a cliche of the worst kind, we are living in a world of change that is absolutely unprecedented in history.

The main impetus behind this rapid change in our society appears to be the genius Americans have; it's probably also our tragedy for being risky enough to take an idea and convert it into action. At no other period in history has there existed such a short period of time between discovery of an idea and its application. Before World War I there was about a thirty-five year lag between the discovery of an idea and its application. Between wars, about seventeen or eighteen years. After World War II, about nine years. If we extrapolate on the basis of those figures, it's about seven years right now between discovery and application. Take, for example, the transistor, which was invented in 1948. Twelve years later it was being used in most of the important hardware in industry. The first industrial application of the computer was in 1956. It's very fashionable now for every organization to be using computer technology. Undoubtedly the laser will experience the same kind of fate as the transistor.

One has to be very pessimistic, however, about drawing a relationship between the rapid change which occurs in technology and the rate of change one can expect in human attitudes and ideas. The technological changes which have taken place in American agricultural methods are profound. But the changes are concrete resulting primarily in greater efficiency. This form of change doesn't seem to interact too much with human attitudes. The key issue of why change in educational systems lags is because it interacts with people.

A second important change reflecting the kind of organizations we live in has to do with the nature of our population. The kinds of people coming into our labor market today are smarter, younger, and more mobile. They're different kinds of people. In fact, the organizations that are growing at the fastest rate right now are vastly different from the organizations that were developing twenty years ago. Nine out of ten people joining the labor force during the last ten years have gone into the service industries—education, health, and welfare. Victor Fuchs indicated in a paper titled "The First Service Economy" that our institutions are moving away from manufacturing to service-oriented kinds of industries which employ different kinds of people.[1] In 1947, for example, approximately fifty-eight million people were employed in service industries as contrasted with seventy-two million at present. Virtually all of this increase occurred in industries that provided services such as banks, hospitals, retail stores, and schools. The number employed in the production of goods has been relatively stable. In 1965, for the first time in the world, our country employed more people in the service industries than in the production of tangible goods. The big problem facing society today is not in large-scale industry and manufacturing but in the management of schools and cities and large-scale service organizations. The nature of our labor market is changing with the result that we're getting more professionals in organizations. In a curious way, organizations of the future are going to resemble school systems. More professional, more highly educated people with different aspirations and who seek different forms of rewards will be employed. Another characteristic of our population is that it is more mobile. Not only is there mobility upward and mobility geographically, but there is also more "intersector mobility." That is, people move from one institution to another more frequently; for example, from education to business or from business to government. As a matter of fact, there was an article in *Fortune* magazine last year called "How to Succeed in Business."[2] The author suggested that one start his career in Washington. He mentioned Keppel, Valenti, and others who went to Washington, then moved on to business. You might use Keppel as the stereotype of the way people are going to move from one institution to another. This is all to be encouraged.

Finally, and this is not too clear to those of us who are studying the changes which affect work relationships, what is required in today's organizations is a different kind of leadership than we've ever known before. As an illustration of this let me refer to the ambassadors and the number two men in the embassies of the Department of State. These men are very wistful for a return to the leadership patterns that they aspired to when they joined the foreign service. That is, they think of themselves as experts who know a good deal about the geopolitics of a certain area. This image of what ambassadorship is supposed to provide in terms of responsibility and position comes partly out of their training. However, an ambassador in the State Department today or a deputy chief of mission is anything but that striped-pants expert in a particular area. Instead, he's at the center of a very complex set of demands, forces, and pressures which are operating on him, transmitting expectations to him, which barely allow him to get to his office to attend to the kind of things that used to occupy the majority of his time. In other words, what he finds himself doing (reluctantly, because he really isn't trained for it) is being an administrator. That is, being at the center of a very complex system which demands coordination, integration, and planning. He is disappointed because these tasks don't meet with his expectations; he feels deprived and he also feels untrained. As a matter of fact, there's a tremendous stereotype in the State Department as in many other institutions, against administration. There is considerable tension in the State Department between people who call themselves "administrators" and people who call themselves foreign service officers. The mutual stereotypes that exist between these two groups is really formidable.

This tension occurs elsewhere as well. Howard Johnson, Dean of the Business School was recently appointed President of M.I.T. The wonder of it, not even a scientist, not even a Ph.D. He was appointed to the position because he was considered a good administrator. The same thing is happening in hospitals. John Knowles, the Director of Massachusetts General Hospital is an administrator. He's effective and successful because he doesn't think administration or managerial competence is a dirty word.

One of the profound problems in professional organization is that when an individual rises in the hierarchy, he finds that he can no longer do the kinds of things that initially attracted him to the organization. Nurses in hospitals, for example, don't want to become nursing supervisors. Their concept of why they went into nursing is to give bedside nursing. It isn't at all rewarding for them to become a nursing supervisor or the head of the nursing service. It is very likely that this same principle holds true as one moves up the hierarchy of a school system.

There is likely to be a sense of deprivation associated with a strong feeling that this is really not a legitimate, respectable thing to be doing.

One cannot be oblivious to the realization that changes are occurring which we had better understand. The demands for running large-scale professional organizations require a massive amount of managerial competence and in many instances this competence cannot be found by promoting people from within. Briefly then, there are four main changes which are affecting organizations: One is the pace and rate of change, which the bureaucratic organization wasn't built to cope with; another is the new kind of organization that we're developing—schools, universities, government, communities, which for a lot of reasons don't seem to be really coordinated with a bureaucratic structure; another is the change in population characteristics. A much different group of people are joining organizations with different aspirations, with different ideas; and fourth, the necessity for possessing managerial competence as well as subsidive competence.

Six Problems Confronting Organizations

It seems appropriate, at this point, to consider the kinds of problems that organizations face, the demands that have been placed on the system, what the bureaucratic solution to that problem was, and to suggest certain solutions that leaders and administrators can utilize. The six areas which are referred to represent some of the main problems that organizations face, as gleaned through a clinical approach to the solution of organizational problems which seem to be interfering with productivity and creativity. They represent, to some extent, most of the research done in the area of industrial social psychology or organizational psychology; and they represent a diagnostic category system of where the problems are. You might reflect on this list to determine if the factors mentioned coincide with your diagnosis of the problems you're experiencing and confronting as a school administrator.

Incentive. The first is the most venerable of almost any problem facing an organization. It has to do with whether or not an individual is getting his kicks from the organization and whether the organization is really getting its share of contributions from the individual. When a person feels he's giving a lot more than he's getting he gets very defensive and starts searching around for new kinds of situations. And when the organization feels he's not contributing his full share, the organization starts doing interesting things about the particular person, like looking for other people to replace him or showing dissatisfaction by not rewarding him. William F. Whyte, Jr. was talking about this problem in his book *The Organizational Man.*[3] In today's large bureaucratic systems the individual isn't really gratifying his own needs; he's become a grey flannel man, bland, indifferent, completely yielding and bending to the organizational pressures. But people do have needs which are complex and changing, however, it's very difficult for leaders and administrators to know what is rewarding to their people. But it's very important that we tune in, particularly in professional organizations, to what is truly rewarding.

The research on incentives for professional people can be summarized in the following way; once given equitable pay, pay is no longer an issue. What is being sought is increased professional enhancement and learning. As a matter of fact, the way to get good people to universities is by developing a super graduate school for the younger men. The older men need different kinds of emoluments, such as ranks, title, and God knows what to make positions attractive. The younger men are looking for a congenial, convivial environment where they can learn and grow.

Professionals in the schools may have different needs. They're not joining a research, teaching, professorial organization. But what do they want? There is some support for the notion that people are using their work these days to develop more personal kicks. People are using work to have peak experiences, to have a good time, through joy and play, and not just to make money. There is a movement in the business community to locate new plants in university towns because that's the way to insure recruitment of young engineers and scientists. A closer relationship is being developed between the universities and industry which is a positive factor in the recruitment of personnel.

Power and its distribution. Given the pressures on administrators such as the president of a university, or a mayor of a city, it is quaint and rustic to think that one man can control, to say nothing of comprehend, the system that he has apparently been given the legal responsibility to direct. This myth of the two-fisted, aggressive, autocratic father leading the enterprise is not only obsolete, it's just not true. There's much more of an executive constellation which is functioning at the head of effective organizations. It's unfortunate that when we assume responsibility we think that we have to possess omnicompetence—which is impossible, given the diversity and complexity of the task. More often, in large organizations the top man, the chief executive, outlines what the major functions

and responsibilities are. He then looks to see where compe-
tencies of various people lie in an attempt to develop some kind
of an executive constellation. Union Carbide, for example, is a
two billion dollar corporation which is run by an executive staff
consisting of five people. It doesn't mean that one man isn't
legally responsible; he is. But it means he needs an awful lot of
help from people at the executive level.

Leadership. One of the studies that Donald Pelz did with
research engineers and scientists had to do with the kinds of
conditions which lead to the most success with respect to the
leadership patterns where they work.[4] He asked people how
they made their important decisions at work; these were mainly
Ph.D.s, scientists, and engineers. Did they make them by themselves exclusively, did the boss make them exclusively, or did
they collaborate with the boss on the decision? He used a
number of measurement devices such as colleague evaluations,
number of patents developed, papers published per year, and so
on to collect data about the productivity of these men. The
data he collected were independent of how the boss thought
about their performance. He established three categories of
performance—high, medium, and low. It turned out that the
lowest performance was obtained when the boss alone made the
decisions. Pelz called this the "deadly condition." High
performers made their decisions in collaboration with their
boss.

One of the biggest blocks to communications in organizations can be subsumed under the problems of power. People
have a difficult time communicating upward. The problem of
communicating downward is not as great. When you're a boss
it's much easier to be open about what's on your mind. But it's
not all that easy to say what's on your mind when you're a

subordinate in an organization. There are a lot of inhibitions and suppressors of upward communication and this quite often means that the most innovative ideas are either not expressed or accepted. As a matter of fact, a good index of an effective, adaptive organization is the extent to which junior people feel that their ideas are being heard and accepted by people above. Where tension or difference exists between people below and above, you have a system that is in trouble. In a situation like that people aren't communicating what's on their mind or volunteering constructive suggestions.

There have been countless studies and experiences showing that when people don't trust their superior, they not only will button up their mouth, but they will also allow people, their bosses, to make mistakes which could be avoided. The best and simple example of this is an experiment that was done by Torrance some years ago in the Air Force.[5] He asked a group of Air Force crews, consisting of captains, lieutenants, and sergeants to solve a simple problem. The problem was called a horse trading problem. A man buys a horse for $80.00, sells it for $90.00, rebuys it for $100.00 and resells it for $110.00. What did he make or lose on the transaction? That's the question. Each group was asked to arrive at the answer by consensus. The interesting thing he discovered was that when the captain had the right answer, in no cases did anybody reject that response. When the lieutenant had the right answer, it was rejected in about 10 per cent of the cases. But when the sergeants had the right answer, it was rejected 30 per cent of the time. Now this probably accounts for only a part of what goes on in organizations where people get conditioned not to speak up, particularly if they think it's something that doesn't agree with what the powers at large believe in. One of the major problems in organizations is working out a system to get more valid innovative information upward. That's a job that all administrators face. Samuel Goldwyn for years led MGM profitably and autocratically. He was known as a tyrant around Hollywood and he was. After a particularly disastrous box-office failure he was said to have called his staff together and remarked, "OK you guys. I want you to tell me exactly what's wrong with the way I'm doing things here at MGM, even if it means losing your job."

The question of collaboration is the most pronounced and the most difficult of the problems facing organizations. It had to do with intergroup conflict and how intergroup conflict in the organization is managed. It's amazing how extensive this problem is and as organizations become more professional there's going to be more of this intergroup fighting. The university is a splendid place to see this at work. In a sense, academic man is at his best in this kind of guerrilla warfare because he stakes out his territory and then fights like hell if anybody encroaches on that area, even if they have better ideas. Robert Hutchins once described the University of Chicago as a peculiar conglomeration of departments, institutes, committees, schools, centers, and programs, all talking their own form of special jargon, largely not communicating, and held together only by a central heating system. That can likely be said about any university system. Being a professional means looking at the world in a certain way. It means that you have a unique view of man. That's what training and education does. It provides what Karl Mannheim once called a "prospectivist orientation." It gives you a way of seeing things differently than most others.

The problem in today's world is that problems don't come labelled economics, psychology, or geography; they don't come packaged as simply as that. As a matter of fact, the real problem

[173]

is to bring professionals from different fields together. People within a professional field often get very threatened when people from other fields begin working on a problem which they feel is unique to their field of study or preparation. It's amazing how little it takes to create extraordinary intergroup competition. As organizations become filled with professionals, as groups become more diverse, real problems develop as to how people can be brought together to work cooperatively. This cooperative, productive endeavor may be referred to as synergy. People with various interests and backgrounds work more productively and more creatively together than they would if they were by themselves. You've seem ball teams that play over their heads. Their success is often credited to high morale. But it's more than that; they turn each other on—collectively.

Most organizations have what we can call a zero synergy strategy. Some organizations even induce competition and negative synergy. Universities, for example, tend to operate primarily on a zero synergy idea. They go about the task of bringing in the best people in the world to organize various departments. These people are given an office and told to go ahead and cultivate their own gardens. So they develop their own turn, their own individuality; they write their papers, and prepare their reports but there is no group effort. It's unfortunate because the solutions to the problems of the future will require a coordinated effort.

Adaptation—an appropriate response to change. There are some people who react stubbornly to new information in different ways. They block the information off, they put it down, or they shelve it. At the other extreme there are people who are overly open, permeable, even spastic about new ideas and information—not that they really internalize it. There are school systems that take on each innovation only to pass it on when the next one comes along. They don't really analyze the purpose behind the idea. Organizations act like this too, in that there is an inappropriate response to innovation—inappropriately open, or inappropriately closed. The question is, how do you get the appropriate response to new information? This is a particularly vexing problem for school administrators. Though change agents are important within an organization, we ought to have a group called counter-change agents who work openly to resist change for change sake. The keen administrator will allow both groups to exist.

Identity. The fifth problem, is the most recent addition to the list. It appears that there are a lot of organizations that seem to be behaving like adolescents and college students; they suffer from an identity crisis. Questions such as these are raised: What are we in the business of doing? Why do we exist as an organization? What's our purpose? It's important to ask these questions periodically and to keep an account of the past because organizations, like individuals can be trapped by the past unless they are aware of it. The point here is that it's important to recognize just what the unique, even primary task of the organization is. It may be simple for a school system, but more likely it is not.

The problem of revitalization. Just as John Gardner has talked about self-renewal for the individual, so too all organizations ought to have some built in agency that spends its time on organizational revitalization.[6] Its main function should be a continual analysis of data from institutional research, and continual concern for transforming, revitalizing, and self-studying. Without it, given the changing times we live in, we're going to back into rather than meet the future head on with a plan to manage and direct what happens in it.

[175]

NOTES

1. Victor Fuchs, "The First Service Economy," *The Public Interest,* No. 2 (Winter, 1966).

2. "How to Succeed in Business, Work in Washington," *Fortune* (March, 1967), pp. 127-133.

3. William F. Whyte, Jr., *The Organizational Man* (New York: Simon and Schuster, Inc., 1956), p. 146.

4. Donald C. Pels, "Freedom in Research," *International Science and Technology* (February, 1964), pp. 55-66.

5. E. P. Torrance, "A Theory of Leadership and Interpersonal Behavior Under Stress," in L. Petrullo and B. M. Bass (eds.), *Leadership and Interpersonal Behavior* (New York: Holt, Rinehart & Winston, Inc., 1961), pp. 100-117.

6. John W. Gardner, *Self Renewal* (New York: Harper & Row, Pub., 1964), pp. 8-20.

11

THE GOVERNANCE OF EDUCATION IN METROPOLITAN AREAS

AUSTIN D. SWANSON

THE ARGUMENTS OF this paper assume the following propositions:

1. *In a democratic society, each citizen should have equal rights before the law.*

2. *In a democratic society, public functions should benefit the general welfare.*

3. *In a democratic society, functions which promote special privilege are inappropriate for support by public institutions and public resources.*

4. *The state has a legitimate concern that each child receive an education which permits him to fulfill his civic and economic responsibilities to society.*

5. *Beyond meeting the basic requirements of the state, the parent has the right to choose the type of schooling his children are to receive within the constraints of his private resources.*

The existing governmental structures for providing public educational services in metropolitan areas are dysfunctional for meeting the educational needs of those areas. Except for limited consolidations of school districts, the basic structures remain virtually unchanged from those which were developed over a century ago when the United States had a small, predominately rural population and an agrarian economy. School government remains geared to those former social and economic conditions despite the fact that the United States is now a large, highly urbanized world power.

Extreme decentralization was required for developing an extensive public school system given the conditions of a century ago. Charles Benson asks:

> Has the decentralized structure of American education been responsible for the extension of educational opportunity? I think the answer is definitely yes. After all, that extension was extremely costly, although, once it is achieved, the continuing burden is unlikely to seem onerous. What our country did, consciously or not, was to exploit local demands for secondary education, with the states giving to local authorities administrative power to extend secondary schooling and at least a modest amount of financial assistance toward that end. The "high school" became a symbol of local pride and hope. But to exploit local demand means that central authority—in this case, the state government—must not raise many questions about standards. The quality of the institutions so established reflected differences in local wealth and in the intellectual backgrounds of local residents. The differences remain remarkable to this day, even though "universal secondary education" had become a reality by the time of World War II.[1]

With the growth of metropolitan areas, the sense of community which fostered local pride and the expansion of public education has diminished. The cities of a century ago, and some not that old, have spilled out of their historic boundaries. Village populations have merged with city populations. Farm lands have been converted into residential neighborhoods, shopping centers, and industrial complexes. The metropolitan growth has even fused the populations of once distant cities into huge megalopolises.

The village population has merged physically with the city population but their governance remains separate. Farm areas have been turned into urban neighborhoods, but they are still governed as farm areas—politically separate from the community of which they are socially and economically a part. The modern American city, unlike the city of a half century ago, is divided into scores (sometimes hundreds) of independent political subdivisions and districts. While these metropolitan areas remain politically divided, sociologists, anthropologists, economists, and urban planners have had to view and analyze their problems in terms of the total natural community.

The very structure which facilitated the development of public education now works to its disadvantage. The technology and economy which has brought people together in metropolitan areas, and permits them to survive there, also places upon them a demand for social and technical skills that can be acquired only through extensive formal education. The day of tolerating inferior education in the name of expansion is past; yet in moving to upgrade inadequate schooling, great caution must be exercised not to level educational services to mediocrity. The quality of all educational services needs to be raised toward the best which the nation's technology can produce and its economy can finance.

The Dysfunctional Nature of Existing
School District Organization

The political boundaries which made good sense a century ago are now being used to promote social and economic causes which are foreign to several of the ideals upon which this nation was established (particularly those propositions noted at the

[179]

beginning of this paper). The nature of the dysfunction is of at least three kinds.

1. Existing governmental structures of metropolitan areas facilitate the use of government to promote islands of privilege and islands of despair.

   a. It divides the community population into politically isolated economic, ethnic, and racial ghettos.

   b. It inhibits upward social mobility and promotes the development of socioeconomic elites.

   c. It deprives the natural community of effective leadership.

2. Existing governmental structures prevent the equitable distribution of the tax resources of the natural community, reinforcing the inequities noted under 1.

3. Existing governmental structures prevent the efficient use of resources of the natural community through their inequitable distribution, the needless proliferation of small units, and the misdirected competition among small units.

Although the disastrous effects of our governmental structure in metropolitan areas did not become fully apparent until following World War II, the seeds were planted early in this century. David Minar notes:

> As a system of social interaction, the city has grown far beyond its earlier confines, a process of growth that, while long under way, has been much accelerated in the years since World War II.

As urban life itself has spread outward from the central city, however, the political structures of the metropolitan area have responded in sluggish and uneven ways. For a period the primary city (the core from which the metropolis grew) expanded its boundaries to keep pace with urban sprawl or altered its nature (as in the creation of Greater New York City) to encompass the metropolitan area. In most parts of the country, political forces at work in state legislatures by the 1920s effectively eliminated annexation as a means of adapting political structure to metropolitan development. This did not, of course, stop the flow of population outward. Thereafter, and to a considerable extent theretofore, the burgeoning suburban areas were freed (or obliged) to find other ways of solving their service needs.[2]

As metropolitan areas grew in population and as technological developments permitted the population to live farther from its work, the higher income groups began to develop neighborhoods outside the central city which catered to their social and economic aspirations. These groups were easily able to capture the political structures of the previously rural communities and they were able to use the powers of government to protect their enclaves. Zoning ordinances were used to protect their investment in real estate and to exclude those of lesser means. Golf courses, parks, and swimming pools were provided for their pleasure through public funds. Public schools were developed which rivaled the most prestigious of private schools. The concern expressed here is not over the nature of these public services, but that they were normally found in adequate quantity and quality only in upper socioeconomic subdivisions of metropolitan areas. When the primary city constituted the metropolitan area, the middle class, in seeking these kinds of services, brought their benefits to all citizens. With the concentration of the middle class in subdivisions politically independent from the primary city, the spill-over effect has been eliminated.

Other rural areas near the central city were taken over by industries. By concentrating industries within small political subdivisions, local property taxes were held at a very low level because of high industrial assessments, coupled with little demand for municipal services from the small residential population.

As the primary cities grew older the tempo of the transition increased. New housing was in the suburbs. Housing in the central city aged and deteriorated. Technological advances made the industrial plants of the city obsolete and it was cheaper for business to relocate in the suburban industrial areas. The automobile and the superhighway freed both industry and labor of locating their plants and their homes in close proximity to one another. The older homes in the primary cities became the residences of the poor.[3] The multistoried factories and warehouses were abandoned. The primary city became a ghetto of lower and lower middle class socioeconomic groups, black and white. The suburbs for the most part became ghettos of the middle and upper middle classes. This process of the upper middle-class population and industries moving to new facilities in previously undeveloped areas is not a new phenomenon. What is new is that these undeveloped areas now lie outside the political jurisdiction of the primary city.

The political situation in the primary cities reinforced the outward movement of the upper middle-class population and of industry. Banfield notes:

> The government of American cities has for a century been almost entirely in the hands of the working class. This class, moreover, has had as its conception of a desirable political system, one in which people are "taken care of" with jobs, favors, and protection, and in which class and ethnic attributes get "recognition." The idea that

[182]

there are values, such as efficiency, which pertain to a community as a whole and to which private interests of individuals ought to be subordinated has never impressed the working class voter.[4]

Contrasting this view, Banfield describes "the ascendant middle-class ideal of government" as "emphasizing 'public values,' especially impartiality, consistency and efficiency."[5]

The philosophical and political division between central city and suburb has developed a cleavage which is not likely to be resolved if cities and suburbs are left to their own resources. For a healthy metropolitan community, there must be dialogue between these factions so that compromise or consensus may take place. For educational matters at least, there is no metropolitan platform where dialogue may take place; the closest platform is the state legislature. Unless metropolitan platforms are developed where educational problems may be studied, debated, and acted upon, these problems will be assumed, probably with less potential effectiveness, by the more remote but more broadly representative legislative bodies in the state capitals and in Washington.

The differences between suburb and central city are not limited to geography or political philosophy. There are also subtle differences working to permanently divide our society. In no circumstances is this more obvious or sinister than with education. The differences between the schools in elite suburban communities and in the central city have been well documented. Expenditures are substantially higher in the suburban communities. It's these communities which are able to attract better qualified teachers. It's these communities where there are the newest facilities and equipment in abundant quantities. It's in these communities where one is most likely to find new instructional techniques being developed and used. Those

[183]

sections of the natural community where the needs are the greatest to overcome the handicap of environment have the least in educational services. But it was not always so. Up to about thirty years ago, prior to extensive suburban development, the schools of the primary city were the prestige schools of an area and the lighthouse schools of the nation.

The subtlety of educational discrimination has been shown by Bruno Bettelheim:

> This intellectual elite will consist of highly educated persons of all colors. Their education and language, their manners and outlook on life will set them apart. They will live and think, act and interact in their own distinctive fashion permanently separated from the rest of the population by education rather than by social or racial barriers.[6]

The separation of our people into ghettos in our metropolitan areas is almost irreversably institutionalized contrary to stated national policies. Yet it is so natural, so human, to attempt to close the gates of personal privilege once one has passed through, thereby improving the probability of success for the children of him who has "arrived" at the expense of the children of him who has not "arrived." Encouraging immediate personal gain has produced a badly divided society which is incapable of working together for the solution of commonly shared problems. The long-term harvest will be bitter for society and for the individual.

Charles Benson writes:

> Decentralization, thus, is no longer consistent with educational expansion, since expansion itself now either connotes impossibly high standards for the smaller local districts to meet—e.g., in establishing junior colleges—or rests upon those kinds of improvements in the quality of elementary programs that local authorities cannot be

expected to provide by their own means. So, while giving all praise to the great work of local school boards for past efforts in extending educational opportunity in this country, let us recognize that the task has now been done, insofar as it lies within the boards' capacities to achieve it. Sentimental attachment to local autonomy should not blind us to the fact that localism may be an inappropriate concept under which to seek higher-quality schooling; and this, not extension *per se,* is the work that faces us in the present in our elementary and secondary schools.[7]

There are those who recognized the problem long before the crisis reached its present critical proportions. Henry C. Morrison wrote in 1943:

The sum of the whole matter seems plainly to be that the school-district system itself is so obsolete, so far removed from the society in which it was once valid, that it has become an incurable malady in our commonwealths.[8]

The problem does not countenance a solution which merely provides for schools which may follow any courses which the vagaries, or the fads, or the ignorance, or the poverty of each of 150,000 different school boards and teaching bodies may dictate. The solution is positive and definite, not opinionative and willful and indeterminate. The task is not more of making it legally and fiscally possible for each of a multitude of local communities "to give *an* education suited to their needs"—or what they think are their needs and what is suited—but rather to guarantee that, so far as is humanly possible and insofar as circumstances do not prohibit, all children shall be put in possession of full General Education.[9]

Restructuring School Government

To restore the integrity of public elementary and secondary education requires a fundamental restructuring of its governance. To guide this revamping, the following are proposed:

[185]

(1) *Any new structure should seek to provide to all persons in a metropolitan area the best quality of educational services which technology can produce and the economy can finance.* The purpose of metropolitan reorganization must be to upgrade educational services for all persons, not to equalize services at a mediocre level. Planners must recognize this natural averaging tendency of large organizations and invent devices for overcoming it. Any proposal which takes substantially from the "haves" and gives to the "have-nots" will fail socially and politically.

(2) *Any new structure for the governance of education in metropolitan areas should promote the social, economic, racial, ethnic, and cultural integration of its population.* Traditionally this has been a principal function of public schools. They were the great national invention for the acculturation of immigrant groups and for the facilitation of upward social mobility by the lower classes. The tendency for school districts in metropolitan areas to encompass relatively homogeneous populations has prohibited public schools from performing this function. Actually the present arrangement accentuates differences rather than reduces them.

(3) *Any new structure must respect existing educational jurisdictions.* This is a matter of practical politics. Existing institutions have strong loyal supporters among their constituents. This is reinforced by vested interests created by historic school district boundaries. Any proposal to arbitrarily legislate these boundaries out of existence will fail politically. A weaning process holds a greater possibility of success whereby people are provided alternatives to the present system among which they may freely choose.

(4) *Any new structure should continue and expand parents' right to choose the type of education they desire for their children.* This has been a traditional right of parents. However, practically speaking, parental option is narrowly restricted. They may send their children to a prescribed public school at no charge; they may send their children to a limited number of private or parochial schools if they can affort the tuition; they may change their residence to a school district more to their liking. Hopefully, a new structure will broaden these very limited options.

(5) *Any new structure should facilitate the efficient and equitable use of metropolitan resources.* From a revenue standpoint this means that local taxation for school support should be levied against the resources of the natural community. From an organizational standpoint this suggests that operating units should be large enough to promote maximum economy of scale.

School districts are no longer necessary. They proved to be extremely successful as an expansionistic tactic. Today the situation is quite different, however. Now there is a strong and general demand for education—stronger than many districts can meet.

At their inception, school districts served natural communities which were relatively isolated from one another. These communities did vary in character and in industry. Their populations were quite stable. Even the immigrants, once arrived, were likely to stay. These factors were used to justify, and indeed required, a substantial degree of local control over curriculum and finance of public schools.

Transportation improvements made it easier for the farmer to get into the village, thereby expanding the natural com-

[187]

munity. Society responded with school consolidation laws which permitted rural school districts to adjust to the new social and economic conditions. Providing equality of educational opportunity in rural schools was the battle cry of the 1920s and 1930s, just as it is in urban schools today.

Transportation, communication, and economic developments have continued to the point where the population is now characterized by mobility, not stability. Most of those who do not change their residences do travel extensively. Mass media are regional and national in character, giving the same exposure to the hinterland as to the metropolis. The same chain stores and the same merchandise are available to the farmer, the city dweller, and the suburbanite. Children are no longer expected to settle down in the community where they were raised. Nor does a retired person necessarily reside in the community where he worked. Nor do those in mid-life work, sleep, shop or play in a single political subdivision. A truly national culture, a national economy, a national technology and a national curriculum have emerged and with them a strong trend toward centralization.

At the same time there has been a trend toward decentralization. Some of the school districts laid out so long ago have come to serve huge school populations. These have proven impossible to manage as monolithic structures. An observable trend has developed of decentralizing certain functions of these bureaucracies.

The nation faces the dilemma of meeting central educational objectives with a decentralized educational structure. Experience reveals that there are serious constraints on the extent to which that structure may be centralized. Experience also reveals that the decentralized structure permits some very harmful inequities. The time has come to carefully examine the supportive functions of public education in order to determine under what conditions each can most effectively be carried out.

Functions which may best be conducted at the metropolitan level—or at the state level—include: establishing general educational objectives and minimum standards, evaluating programs against minimum standards, securing necessary financial resources, conducting area planning, coordinating educational services of operating units, reviewing and approving budgets of operating units, providing facilities, determining salaries, purchasing supplies, and transporting children.

Functions which can best be handled at the operating unit level are those of an implementive nature. These would include: establishing specific educational objectives, designing or adapting programs for meeting those objectives, evaluating programs against specific objectives, developing operating budgets (allocating resources to specific programs), planning the educational plant, selecting personnel, educating children.[10]

Certain state universities, including the University of California and the State University of New York, provide prototypes of public educational institutions which divide their functions in a fashion similar to that suggested above. These institutions have a single policy-making and coordinating body, yet operationally they rely on scores of quasi-independent components scattered about their respective states. Translating this structure into one for providing public elementary and secondary education in metropolitan area schools would mean the further centralization of certain functions, especially the revenue function, and the decentralization of other functions, especially the administration of instruction. Simply, the plan would

[189]

involve the creation of a metropolitan educational agency responsible for the overall planning and coordinating for education in the metropolitan area and for providing the necessary revenue; the elimination of school district boundaries but the retention of operational agencies similar to present school boards; and the elimination of attendance areas but the retention of instructional agencies similar to present day schools. The metropolitan agency would receive some of the powers now given to school boards such as taxation and facility construction, plus additional powers which are needed but not presently assumed by any educational agency. The operating units would inherit most of the powers of the present day school board except those reassigned to the metropolitan agency. The instructional units would not be greatly altered, except that they would be given more autonomy in matters of curriculum, organization, and personnel selection.

The metropolitan board. The metropolitan board of education would be responsible for the general planning, developing and financing of educational services in the area. The metropolitan board would construct and hold title to all facilities within its jurisdiction. As the population expands, the board would be responsible for chartering new operational units or expanding existing ones. They could also directly administer or establish special purpose agencies for the providing of highly specialized services. It is conceivable that metropolitan museums, libraries and performing art groups could be placed under its jurisdiction.

The metropolitian board would have the authority to levy taxes and to receive state and federal financial assistance. Operational units would not have such authority. (This would greatly simplify the allocation of state financial assistance, at

[190]

least to metropolitan areas, since the necessity of the "equalization" function of state aid would be largely removed and the number and variety of units with which the state deals would be sharply reduced.) The metropolitan board would receive and evaluate the budgetary requests of the operating units and other component agencies. Allocation decisions would be made according to Planning, Programming, Budgeting procedures (PPBS).

The operating unit. The operating unit could take on a variety of organizational patterns, most of which are yet to be invented. The number of children served could vary from a few up to a maximum of approximately 25,000. Each operating unit would be governed by a board of trustees. No unit would serve a specific attendance area. Parents would be permitted to select the unit they wished their children to attend. A parent would have the option of withdrawing his child from one unit and enrolling him in another. On the other hand, a child moving within the metropolitan area need not necessarily change units. These arrangements would inject into public education a spirit of competition and experimentation which is now unfortunately lacking.

Publicly finance transportation would be scheduled by the metropolitan board of education for children attending schools beyond walking distance from their homes. When admission requests to an operating unit exceed the available spaces, selection would be made by lottery. After admitting a child, the unit would be obligated to provide him a space as long as he wished to remain. In order to preserve the integrative function of public education, it would be necessary to stratify enrollment spaces in each unit according to family income, a primary indicator of socioeconomic status. Such structuring would also serve the social purpose of racially integrating the units.

The central administration of the unit would be responsible for the overall planning, developing and coordination of the unit's educational program. Each school within the unit, however, would be free, and even encouraged, to develop its own educational programs. Until the superiority of one educational approach over others can be clearly demonstrated, variety, not uniformity, is in order. This independence of program would be reinforced in the financial planning for parks through the use of Planning, Programming, Budgeting systems (PPBS).[11] Resources would be allocated to schools on the basis of the rationale of requests in terms of objectives, programs and results. The unit's central administration would bear the responsibility for evaluating the programs of its schools in the light of stated unit-school objectives. The central administration would also be responsible for consolidating the programs and financial requests of the schools and of the central services into a budgetary request to the metropolitan board of education.

The instructional units. The operating units would consist of schools similar to the common neighborhood school but with greater program independence from the central administration of the operating unit.Once again variety and evaluation would be encouraged through a PPB system. Funds would be allocated by the operating units to the instructional units using such a system.

A Transitional Plan

Transition to such an arrangement can be made through a gradual non-disruptive process. An immediate step would be the establishment of a metropolitan board of education.[12] Title to all public school property in the metropolitan area would be turned over to this board along with all outstanding debt. Only the metropolitan board (and the state board) would have the authority over approving and financing future construction. The metropolitan board would develop a master plan for educational services along the lines described above and move toward its implementation. Responsibility for all school transportation also would be assigned to this board.

Existing school districts would be permitted to continue to operate their systems as at present (except for construction and transportation) or they could dissolve and turn their operation over to the metropolitan board. The metropolitan board would assign the schools (instructional units) of dissolved districts to various board-chartered operating units.

Districts continuing to operate schools would retain taxing authority for operating expenses. Their students would have the right to attend any school administered by the metropolitan board subject to the limitations listed above in addition to those operated by the district. The school district would have to pay tuition to the metropolitan board for students electing metropolitan schools. Metropolitan board taxes for capital purposes would be levied on the entire metropolitan area. Metropolitan board taxes for operating purposes would be levied only in those areas where the school districts had been dissolved. Appropriate adjustments would be required in state financial aid programs.

The option to continue existing school districts would probably be exercised primarily by upper middle-class suburbs. These are the districts which have prospered most under the present structure. One of the criteria established earlier was that the level of education for all children be raised. In order to assure this, the best of today's schools must be permitted to continue. The degree to which the new operating units can lure students away from today's prestige districts will be a measure of their quality.

It is anticipated that virtually all school districts would in time voluntarily turn over their responsibilities to the metropolitan board. Quality control would consist of systematic evaluation of ongoing programs, an integral part of PPBS, and competition engendered by an expansion of parental choice options.

The above proposal would convert an agrarian concept of public education (school districts and neighborhood schools) into one which is designed for modern metropolitan conditions. It would enable publicly supported schools to perform once again their integrative and social mobility functions. The built-in quality control features would insure all persons in the metropolitan area access to a quality of educational services equal to, or exceeding, the best of that which is now available. This would be accomplished without arbitrarily destroying the existing structure. Parental right to choose the type of schooling for their children would be greatly enhanced. Metropolitan resources would be more generally available and their use would be made more efficient through area-wide coordination.

NOTES

1. Charles S. Benson, *The Cheerful Prospect* (Boston: Houghton Mifflin Co.), p. 14.

2. David Minar, "Instruction of School and Local Non-School Governments in Metropolitan Areas," in *Metropolitanism Its Challenge to Education—The Sixty-Seventh Yearbook of the National Society for the Study of Education* (Chicago: University of Chicago Press, 1968), p. 199.

3. Older structures have always been abandoned to the poor. It is economically not possible to build new housing that the poor can afford without subsidization. This traditional behavior has reinforced the ghettoization of our metropolitan areas in that virtually all of the old structures are in the primary city and virtually all of the new structures are in the suburbs. Before the primary city had saturated its political boundaries, both new and old structures were available within them.

4. Edward C. Banfield, "The Political Implications of Metropolitan Growth," *Daedalus* XC (Winter, 1961), p. 70.

5. *Ibid.,* p. 73.

6. Bruno Bettelheim, "Segregation: New Style," *The School Review,* LXVI, No. 3 (Autumn, 1958), 264.

7. Benson, *op. cit.,* pp. 17-18.

8. Henry C. Morrison, *American Schools* (Chicago: University of Chicago Press, 1943), p. 266.

9. *Ibid.,* p. 282.

10. Dr. Henry M. Brickell has made a similar suggestion in his paper "Local Organization and Administration of Education," in Edgar L. Morphet and Charles O. Ryan (eds.), *Designing Education for the Future No. 2—Implications for Education of Prospective Changes in Society* (New York: Citation Press, 1967), pp. 221-222.

11. Hartley defines program budgeting as relating "the output-oriented programs, or activities, of an organization to specific resources that are then stated in terms of budget dollars. Both programs and resources are projected for at least several years into the future. Emphasis is upon outputs, cost-effectiveness methods, rational planning techniques, long range objectives and analytical tools for decision making." See Henry J. Hartley, *Educational Planning—Programming—Budgeting* (Englewood Cliffs, N.J.: Prentice-Hall, Inc., 1968). See also David Novick (ed.), *Program Budgeting, Program Analysis and the Federal Budget* (Cambridge, Mass.: Harvard University Press, 1967).

12. Another transitional alternative would be for the state board of education to charter and to directly finance and supervise elementary and secondary schools or larger complexes such as educational parks which would compete for students with

existing school districts. Such schools could enrol students from anywhere in the metropolitan area. The district of residence of students attending these schools would be charged tuition. This arrangement would accomplish many of the objectives of the transitional plan presented in the tax but it would constitute direct state intervention and would provide little coordination of metropolitan educational planning or of the use of resources.

12

URBAN SCHOOL ADMINISTRATION— SOME PROBLEMS AND FUTURES

TROY V. McKELVEY

THIS REPUBLIC HAS been rapidly transformed into an urban society. All areas of society—economic, social, political—reflect this increasing rate of change, and the problems associated with it. Urban centers are now struggling for their very existence. The change in the overall society from rural to urban cannot help but increase the demands upon urban educational administrators. Problems of negotiation, desegregation, finance, and community demands for increased services can be identified daily by the urban school administrator—be he superintendent or building principal.

The Context and Nature of Urban Education

It would be easy to write a scathing indictment of urban school administration—its bulky bureaucracy, its slowness to change, its seemingly defensive attitude about its present programs and activities. Such indictments have been written by minority groups and scholars striving for quality educational programs. They are a matter of record in every major city system. To accuse, however, is less productive than to examine major issues and problems facing urban school administrators. One major problem lies at the base of urban education—the school systems' inadequate response to change. Changes outside the organizational structure of the urban school system have been so rapid that the system itself has been unable to adapt to them.

The urban administrative system has been lacking in its ability to change its own structure and become a self-renewing system. The self-renewing nature of an educational system is more than innovation and change. "It is also the process of bringing the results of change into line with our organizational purposes."[1] Self-renewal demands long-range planning, the ability to see around the corner, and the promise of updating and of rejuvenating the system on a continuous basis. Urban school systems have been less than adequate in their adoptions of such concepts as they apply to their organizational structures.

The purposes of education in urban America are in need of examination. The question is will the existing structure of education allow this examination to take place? It has been said that "the greatest resistance to change comes from man's compulsion to be tied to existing organizational structures." This adherence to the stereotype behavior of a hierarchy will continue as long as it is within the normative expectations of the organization and in the larger culture.

The Plight of the Urban System

If one were to peruse school board minutes of large cities in the late 1800s, one would find that city schools originally were

[198]

organized for purposes other than solely educating youth. The bulging industry of the city brought on an increasing amount of markcting and commcrcial activity. Children of these cities literally were getting in the way. Newspaper accounts of that period state that children were being run over by wagons or trampled by horses, and in many cases were disrupting the commercial interaction in the market place. Schools in most urban centers, therefore, were originally created as custodial institutions. Such school systems, as they became organized, took on the cloak of the organizational structure used in Western and Central European schools of that period. This formal and the ensuing informal structure which developed have remained basically unchanged.

Urban building programs of the nineteenth century were part of a larger pattern of growth. Many buildings presently being used in some urban centers were built before 1900. Although many others have been built since, appropriate financing for remodeling and renewal of older school facilities has been lacking.

As the administrative structures of urban schools developed, they moved toward a strong bureaucracy similar to the political structure which existed in the city, and more often than not, the office of the superintendent of schools became a part of that structure. Although education had a separate board, it was usually appointed by the mayor. The general attitude of the superintendent was that in order to survive, he had to pay particular attention to the political structure. School budgets usually were at the mercy of the city legislative councils. Demands were also increasing for many other city services—fire, police, and sanitation. Consequently, school building programs for remodeling or new construction and, for that matter, the support for educational programs in general, usually held a low priority. (Evidence of such behavior on the part of city governments is apparent in Buffalo, New York, presently in need of ninety million dollars to update its school building program. Only half this is needed for new construction.) One can conclude that some problems of urban administration can be attributed to the internal political structure, the increasing demand for city services other than education, and a general negative attitude toward educational expenditures.

It is almost trite to reiterate that urban school systems in general are operating on a declining tax base. Most large cities are blessed with several interesting situations: low assessed valuation, constitutional limits for property taxation, and an increasing amount of property being withdrawn from the tax rolls. In many cities one can see, immediately adjacent to the inner city, miles and miles of large homes which have been purchased by non-profit organizations and are not subject to the property tax.

Only a few of the financial difficulties of the big cities have been discussed. Their buildings are old, their maintenance costs are high, they are operating on a narrowing tax base and in most situations are constrained by the attitudes of the political structure. In addition to these financial problems, cities are faced with heavier costs for technical-vocational training and program improvement in general. Land is becoming more expensive, and in many large cities, a greater proportion of teachers are at the top of the salary schedule. The combination of these factors indeed makes the plight of big city school administration a grievous one. Can the city solve this problem without assistance from other governmental sources? Many think not. The increasing interest of industry in accepting some responsibility for curing this social ill is heartening. Federal support for personnel development will soon be available. The combined efforts of both the public and private sectors of the economy are needed.

While discussing some of the major issues emerging in urban school administration, we might well look at some of the expectations and responsibilities of urban school administration and the relationships between them. Such role relationships exist between the board and the superintendent, between the superintendent and the staff, between the central office staff and the building principal, between the building principal and his teaching staff and the client system; the students, parents, and laymen who make up his attendance area. Broadly speaking, urban school administration can be classified in three distinct sections: (1) The board of education, responsible for broad policy-making for the entire system, (2) the superintendent and his staff, usually responsible for central office administration for the total district, and (3) the building principals, representing the administrative leadership in each attendance area. These three entities make up the administration of the urban school district. The following discussion takes note of the present situation and some possible futures for each of these categories.

The Board of Education

Traditionally, boards of education have been looked upon by the general public as their representatives in charge of schools. Theoretically and according to state law, boards of education exist to represent the people in the formulation of broad policy concerning the education of children within the district. A

[201]

school board is also a representative arm of the state, for education is a function and a responsibility of the state. The fact that urban boards of education arc both elective and appointive has from time to time been contested, resulting in very strong points of view concerning school board selection. The argument seems to be running stronger for the elective boards. However, this argument is far from settled. There is little basic evidence which would weight the scale one way or the other. The majority of school board members in a recent study prefer the method by which they were selected. This study also points out that the behavior of school boards toward integration is dependent upon the recruitment process which varies with the presence of economic elites, strong political structures and low status populations.[2] School board members find themselves in an interesting situation, with expectations from the public for controlling public education and without remuneration for their services. This fact alone has caused some difficulty in recruitment from a broad representative base.

Boards of education have recently come under extreme criticism, especially on the issue of desegregation. Some might contend that boards of education in large urban centers have been less than representative of the people they are supposed to represent. This point finds much support, in the rising conflict with minority groups. There seems to be a large portion of the urban community that finds itself not represented. Boards of education have become increasingly aware of pressure groups within and without the community and though their responsibility is to establish broad policy, it should be pointed out that some boards of education have busied themselves with trivialities and the particularistic tasks of operating a school system in lieu of studying and developing broad policy which would improve the operation of the entire school system.

Some large school systems have been guided toward an emphasis on particularistic arrangement rather than policy formation. It is impossible for boards to develop policy if they are bogged down in the trivialities of counting ketchup bottles or deciding the size of brooms to be used by custodians.[3] To be sure, the behavior of boards of education forms a continuum from broad policy development to the actual administration of schools. However, it would seem that by this time we would have developed compatible and common expectations for school board members and the actions of responsible school boards. The American School Board Association has come a long way in its goal of accomplishing the proper role of boards of education, but unfortunately, in some school systems, there is still a long way to go. It is indeed unfortunate that criticism directed at members of boards of education may act as a constraint upon potential board members. One of the strong constraints against talented laymen emerging within the community to accept board of education positions or to place themselves for election may result from this strong criticism and the lack of remuneration for their efforts. They are in the eyes of many remunerated in many other ways. One begins to wonder if such responsible positions should not be more legitimately compensated in light of their overall effect upon education. One questions whether the concept of volunteerism still applies in the selection of school board members. The need is for highly competent, thoroughly educated, humanistic individuals who can set the guidelines for the operation of our schools. It may well be impossible to correct the ills of our present urban systems under old guidelines, old policies, and time-worn ideas not suited to today's urban setting. In the future, school boards will survive only if our knowledge increases concerning the responsibilities of such deliberative bodies and if school board members discipline themselves in the performance of those responsibilities.[4]

The obvious link to the board of education is the superintendent of schools. A prime duty of a board of education is to select a superintendent—the administrative head of the school system. One might expect boards of education to choose top administrative heads somewhat compatible with the thinking of the board. This compatibility, however, is less than a fact in today's central cities, where superintendents are appointed by a slim majority vote and feel themselves comfortable to have 5-4 or 4-3 votes on many issues coming before their board. Many enter their positions with a fair number of board members dissenting their appointments. Consequently, new policy formulations within school districts hang on a narrow margin for or against adoption.

The Superintendent and His Staff

Normally, the superintendent has a staff of several associate superintendents, assistant superintendents, and a number of directors. He alone, however, is responsible for the administration of schools throughout the system. Superintendents have always received a certain amount of criticism. However, this criticism has increased in our cities to the point where some very good men have been forced to leave this important post before their programs for change could be initiated and disseminated throughout the system. Though it is true that the tenures of the large city superintendents have been somewhat brief, it is also true that a new breed of large city superintendent is emerging. This master administrator, having the opportunity to fill important staff positions with people from both inside and outside the system, may effect change in the near future to enable a central school system to be self-initiating, self-evaluating, and self-renewing. There is little doubt that superintendents of today's urban centers must have tough skins,

[204]

able to take criticism and the conflict that surrounds their office and permeates their system. However, today's superintendent must, more than ever before, also be highly perceptive, sensitive, and humanistic in his behavior and have the ability to conceptualize problems. Though he may be a perceptive generalist, he cannot be expected to be a specialist and an expert in all facets of today's administration. Surely, he must have some broad knowledge of communications, human relations, and the educational technology available. He is expected to have knowledge of the theory and broad principles involved in every facet of administration. Today's superintendent hires competent staffs who specialize in the particulars of a given area. He will hire the communications specialist, the systems analyst, the computer technologist as resources to administration. These men of specialty assist the superintendent in dealing with the particulars of broad principles introduced into a system. Many new careers are emerging in the administration of urban school systems. For example, some districts are intensifying the planning process. Planners and developers have long been a part of building programs in educational systems. However, now the organizational planner, or systems analyst, emerges to assist the superintendent in evaluating and restructuring the very system of which he is the head. Large educational organizations have long been known for their bottlenecks and disconnected communications systems, with people at the top not knowing what the people at the bottom are doing. This is characteristic of all large bureaucratic systems. The emerging specialist will ferret out the dysfunctional aspects of a system, define new subsystems in lieu of old ones, and thus reformulate the system according to its changing needs and objectives.

The superintendent's position, though significantly important, is a lonely one. This has been attested to by many consultants in their private conversations and discussions with large city superintendents. In many situations the superintendent really has few people to talk to and in some cases, fewer still whom he can trust. Some superintendents have become the virtual guardians of all information fed in or out of the system. This is understandable, for information in the past has been used against them by those opposed to change. Such behavior tends to create a closed system. It is however, more important to open the system than to close it. Rather than to be so defensive about the wrongs in a system, it might be well to admit them and to be more diligently seeking their elimination. Many would say that administrators of central cities have swept problems under the rug for too long. It is highly unlikely that this behavior resolves the problem. Intensifying the risk-taking component of leadership and the modification of the constraints of finance and organizational structure could improve the situation.

Aside from the central office staff, today's urban superintendent, depending on the size of the school district, has a large group of building principals. The principal's role is ever increasing in its importance to the total system and to the education of children. Here is "where the tire hits the pavement." Here is where the action is.

The Building Principal

"As goes the principal, so goes the school," is not a trite phrase. It can be supported by several studies completed in urban centers. Studies implemented to assist large city school systems in establishing priorities for change have identified innovative programs. They also find innovative principals initiating these programs. Unfortunately, such programs are few and far between. In many cases the building principal in the urban system is a product of the system. Constraints of procedure developed to regulate the identification, and the appointment of principals, has a tendency to delay advancement to the principalship. In most large systems teachers are required to complete a specified number of years as a classroom teacher; the next rungs of the ladder are to become qualified by passing examinations, and to be placed on a waiting list. From the waiting list, one moves to the vice-principalship; time in office is required at each level in the succession. In some systems ten to twelve years of service is required to become principal. This procedure is being questioned by some as being too lengthy and relying too greatly on experience. Although most systems require both experience and training, length of experience is in question. How many years should a budding administrator be an assistant principal before he takes over the reins of leadership? How many years should a classroom teacher teach before being eligible for a principalship? Answers to these questions are not readily available, but they remain in need of examination.

The new principal in an urban setting enters the principalship with a great deal of enthusiasm but he soon finds that the constraints of the system curtail and delay his efforts. As a consequence, many central building principals find their behavior maintains the system rather than changing and improving it. Too many, I fear, are identified as outstanding principals, are elevated to central office positions, and then co-opted into another career. It has been said, but not supported by central office personnel, that elevation to the central office of the innovative administrator or building principal may well be the first stage of retirement.

Is the building principal trained to cope with the problems of today in urban schools? Is the training and experience appropriate for today's conflicts and for today's decision-making? Is the situation of the urban principal analogous to the statement recently made by the Police Commissioner of New York City in referring to the policemen as being inadequately trained for the new developments in our cities? Few urban school systems have been without in-service training for teachers. It is, however, disappointing to note the small number of in-service programs designed for administrators at the building level. Retraining has become a part of almost every administrative facet of industry. Why has it been delayed so long in our urban school systems?

A systematic program for retraining is essential for both secondary and elementary building principals. New developments in the field of administration and new problems associated with administering urban schools have placed even the role of the principal in jeopardy. Not only has his client system changed but the behavior of those clients has changed. The behavior of the teaching staff has changed. What happens to the building principal's authority when teachers now negotiate directly with boards of education for salary increases? Has not the authority of the principal been circumvented? Some would say that the principal's authority no longer rests with his position. The future of the building principal will most likely rest in his competence for initiating new programs, dealing more effectively with people, and proving to his teaching staff that he can provide services which they sorely need.

A modern day principal in an urban setting can no longer pass the buck. The case in the past had been that he passed problems on to the central office. This is one of the reasons why urban superintendents have such short tenure. The superintendent has been the sole person responsible for decisions within the district. One way of alleviating this problem would be to grant increasing autonomy to the building principal and holding him accountable for his actions. Some districts are now experimenting with allowing the building principal to make decisions about all areas of finance and staff utilization. In such districts the building principal is given, in accordance with a formula, the district average teacher's salary for each teacher unit in his building. The principal in turn is able to hire teachers and teacher-aides in accordance with his needs or in accordance with an organizational structure to best carry out those needs. The building principal must be increasingly aware of the constituents of his attendance area. He can no longer accept the stereotypes of the past, for his community is in a constant state of change. Processes of community relations are far more sophisticated now than even five years ago. The development of qualities inherent in good human relations and the skills in dealing with conflicts must become a part of all training and retraining programs for urban school administrators. The problems of building administration based on yesterday's assumptions are becoming very acute. One can hardly pick up a city newspaper without reading of an organization attacking the principal of a school. Such attacks, whether verbal or written, can more than likely be based on a breakdown or lack of some component in the system.

Building principals in city systems have become quite defensive which is not uncharacteristic of most city school personnel. Defensiveness is understandable. First of all, city systems develop an image, whether accurate or not, of being poor educational systems. This is brought about by a usual good image of the surrounding suburban school district; one might guess that neither of these images is true, that in fact there are many

[209]

sound educational programs in both urban and suburban systems. However, no one likes to live with a poor image; thus, the defensive behavior. Such defensiveness, however, cannot be rationalized on inaction or behavior that tends to be maintenance-oriented. When visiting building principals, one sometimes recalls the county extension agent who visited the farmer, and the farmer said, "Don't give me any of those new-fangled ideas. I'm not presently farming half as good as I know how."

The analogy may not be the best, for it infers a sense of knowing. Many of today's urban superintendents say it is difficult to find quality leadership at the building level. Some blame the colleges for not training this leadership. Large city superintendents cannot find principals trained to deal with the problems of the inner core of metropolitan areas.[5] Yet, through relentless and continued efforts of the county agricultural agent, the behavior of the farmer did change. The dissemination and use of modern agricultural techniques is today a fact and is supported by increased productivity.

Urban Teachers

Recently the question was asked, "How can the principal help the members of the faculty to redirect their attitudes, planning, and procedures so as to provide better educational opportunities for all children?"[6] The fact that this question concerns "redirection" suggests that the attitudes, planning and procedures of at least some teachers are not what they should be.

Inner city teachers of the past and present have the problems of quality control and staying power. How can high quality teachers be recruited to the inner city schools and how can these teachers be encouraged to stay? The inner city school has been unattractive to teachers seeking recognition and having divergent value patterns. Teaching has been attractive in the inner city to some because of the apathy of administrators and parents.[7] Neither the rationale of the "stayers" or the "leavers" can be tolerated. Inner city schools cannot remain centers of watered down curriculums or the sanctuaries for those who wish to teach in obscurity.

The future will soon see a new breed of teacher entering the inner city school. Programs of early recruitment and commitment have been underway at many teacher-training institutions. Observation, practice teaching and internships begin and continue in the inner city school. Methods classes are taught in the public school rather than in college classrooms. Much of the activity mentioned above has dealt with the slum school which is a black school. But what of the consequences of new integration policies recently placed in motion by many urban school systems? Are we preparing experienced and new teachers to cope with the problems of these newly integrated schools? Some are far less concerned about the new teacher in this regard. For it is the teacher of experience who may fail to understand or have the attitude of tolerant understanding necessary for peaceful and meaningful integration.

Teachers in urban schools must know the students well. To know them well is to know their homes and parents. As the parents of the urban school become more education conscious and organize themselves within their communities, both teachers and building administrators will be pressed to create new ways of communicating and negotiating conflict. Parents have always been a threat to teachers whether in urban or suburban settings. However, where intensified and well organized efforts have been undertaken to bring parents and teachers together, the results have been gratifying. In the Banneker District in St. Louis, teachers found their fears to be unwarranted and better education resulted for the children of the district when a program of home visitation was initiated (see Shepard, chapter 7).

Of course there are islands of educational activity where severe criticism is not appropriate but they remain small islands indeed.

The Clients

The future is most often difficult to predict; however, it takes little insight to predict that organized criticism and pressure will be exerted and increased on the urban school. For teachers and administrators to draw lines of battle is a mistake. The clients, both parents and students of urban schools have long thought of the institution we call a school as the enemy. Why reinforce this prevailing attitude? The school is a part of the establishment and is likely to remain so until the client system sees some results of their newly-expressed demands.

Too many administrators are still asking the time-worn question: what do black parents want for their children? The answer is simple. Blacks want the same things from the educational enterprise that whites want for their children. Busing is also an issue in the black community. Recently a black mother from the Roxbury District in Boston said, "If you think I am busing my child to suburbia so that he can sit next to a white child, you're crazy. I'm busing my child because I believe he will receive a better education in the suburbs." Opening opportunities for busing or open enrollment in urban settings will increase ghetto parent protest of inadequate facilities and irrelevant curriculums. Parental involvement in education is on the increase and will continue to be until actions speak louder than words.

Direct conflict between teachers and parents is on the increase. When organized teachers and organized parents are a party to conflicts which can close a school system the size of New York City, the situation becomes critical. The emergence of parental force and participation in policy formation may be constructive as well as unsettling. The New York experience exemplifies the fact that, "Organized parents, even if they are clear about their aims, cannot achieve more direct controls over the school or the school system in the absence of cooperation with teacher groups."[8]

Through the confusion that presently exists concerning the integration of our urban school systems, be they North or South, few predictions of the future are possible. Research and study of the complexities surrounding the issue are now emerging but to speak with certainty is presumptuous.[9] A system of designing educational organizations and their components, evaluating their utility, and disseminating the resulting knowledge should be of highest priority for the total educational enterprise of our nation. The die is cast; the relevance of education as it now exists is being challenged. Administrators are found wanting in the ability to lead the school system in coping with these challenges. New models for organizing education, which are relevant to its characteristics, must replace the inadequate hierarchical model of today.

[213]

NOTES

1. John, W. Gardner, *Self-Renewal* (New York: Harper & Row, Pub., 1964).

2. Robert L. Crain, *The Politics of School Desegregation* (Chicago: Aldine Pub. Co., 1968), chaps. 12 and 13.

3. Joseph Pois, *The School Board Crisis* (Chicago: Educational Methods, Inc., 1965).

4. Keith Goldhammer, "Local Provisions For Education," in Edgar L. Morphet and David L. Jesser (eds.), *Emerging Designs for Education* (Denver: Designing Education For the Future, 1968).

5. Keith Goldhammer *et al., Issues and Problems in Contemporary Educational Administration* (Eugene, Oregon: The Center for the Advanced Study of Educational Administration, University of Oregon, 1967).

6. D.E.S.P. *The Elementary School Principalship in 1968* (Washington, D.C.: The Department of Elementary School Principals, N.E.A., 1968).

7. William W. Wayson, "Securing Teachers for Slum Schools," *Integrated Education* (February/March, 1964). Reprinted in Meyer Weinberg (ed.), *Integrated Education* (Beverly Hills: Glencoe Press, 1968). See also William W. Wayson, "Expressed Motives of Teachers in Slum Schools," *Urban Education,* I (1965), and "Sources of Teacher Satisfaction in Slum Schools," *Administrators Notebook,* (1966).

8. Weinberg, *op. cit., Introduction.*

9. T. Bentley Edwards and Frederick M. Wirt, *School Desegregation in the North* (San Francisco: Chandler Pub. Co., 1967).

The Authors . . .

TROY V. McKELVEY—*Assistant Professor of Education, State University of New York at Buffalo.* In addition to his teaching assignments, Dr. McKelvey is a Council Associate to the Western New York School Study Council. A specialist in elementary school organization, he was Post Doctoral Fellow at the Center for the Advanced Study of Educational Administration, University of Oregon, prior to joining the faculty of the State University of New York at Buffalo. He was a Teaching Fellow in the Division of Educational Administration, School of Education, University of California, Berkeley, where he received an Ed. D. degree.

AUSTIN D. SWANSON—*Associate Professor of Education, State University of New York at Buffalo.* In addition to his teaching assignments, Dr. Swanson is Council Associate to the Western New York School Study Council. Prior to joining the faculty at the State University of New York at Buffalo he was a Research Associate with the Institute of Administrative Research, Teachers College, Columbia University, where he received the Ed. D. degree. A specialist in public school finance, he served as the Executive Secretary of the Central School Boards Committee for Educational Research.

SAUL ALINSKY—*Director of the Industrial Areas Foundation.* Mr. Alinsky graduated from the University of Chicago with a bachelor's degree and later returned to pursue graduate work in criminology. His professional career includes working as a sociologist with the Institute for Juvenile Research and organizing slum areas in several American cities. Mr. Alinsky became a national figure when he organized a Negro slum in the Chicago Woodlawn area. His more recent organizational efforts have been in the cities of Rochester and Buffalo. Mr. Alinsky has published widely, contributing numerous articles in the profes-

[216]

sional journals of sociology, criminology, and psychology.

WARREN G. BENNIS—*Provost of the Faculty of Social Sciences and Administration, State University of New York at Buffalo.* Prior to his present appointment, Dr. Bennis was Chairman of the Organization Studies Group at the Massachusetts Institute of Technology's Sloan School of Management and Professor of Organizational Psychology and Management. He has served as visiting lecturer in Social Relations at Harvard University and the University of Southern California. Dr. Bennis has served as an international professor and project director in Switzerland and India. He received his Ph.D. at M. I. T. and has studied at the London School of Economics. Dr. Bennis has published widely in his field, and has made major leadership contributions to many professional associations. He is an internationally recognized scholar of organizational behavior, having written or edited over 10 books and 100 articles on leadership, motivation, and change in large scale, complex organizations. His latest book, entitled *The Democratic Revolution,* will be published by Harper and Row in 1969.

DAVID K. COHEN—*Research Associate, Center for Educational Policy Research, Graduate School of Education, Harvard University.* He was previously Director of the Race and Education Study conducted by the United States Commission on Civil Rights. Prior to his appointment on that study, Dr. Cohen was Assistant Professor in the Department of Social Science and Humanities at the Case Institute of Technology. His professional experience includes being a consultant to national church and civil rights organizations. Dr. Cohen received his Ph.D. in Sociology from the University of Rochester and has published widely in professional journals in areas of sociological theory and school segregation.

FRANK J. DRESSLER–*Associate Superintendent of the Buffalo Public Schools.* Dr. Dressler's professional experience includes both teaching and administration. He has lectured in Political Science at Millard Fillmore College and has taught at State University College at Buffalo. Dr. Dressler is a member of the Task Force on School University Teacher Education being sponsored by the Research Council of the Great Cities Improvement Program. He has also served as a consultant to the President's Council on Vocational Education and the United States Office of Education.

MARIO D. FANTINI–*Program Director, Ford Foundation.* In addition to teaching at all levels of education, Dr. Fantini taught and directed programs for the retarded and disadvantaged. He has directed experimental programs in teacher education and was chairman of the General Education Program for Teachers and the Intern Teacher Training Program in Special Education at Temple University. Dr. Fantini received a certificate for advanced study in educational administration and an Ed. D. from Harvard University. Prior to joining the Ford Foundation he served as Senior Research Associate, directed the Madison Area Project, and the Urban Teacher Preparation Program, at Syracuse University. Dr. Fantini has directed projects sponsored by the National Institute of Mental Health, United States Office of Education, and the Ford Foundation. He has served as a consultant to the mayors of several major cities. Dr. Fantini has written many articles appearing in professional journals, and is co-author of *The Disadvantaged: Challenge to Education.*

R. OLIVER GIBSON–*Professor of Education, State University of New York at Buffalo.* Dr. Gibson, prior to joining the faculty of the State University of New York at Buffalo, was a lecturer in education and a Research Associate at Harvard University, where he received his Ed. D. degree. He has served as Master at Mount Allison Academy and Commercial College and Superintendent of Schools in Nova Scotia, Canada. In addition to his present University teaching assignments, Dr. Gibson is a consultant to the Chicago Public Schools. Most noteworthy of his publications is *The School Personnel Administrator,* co-authored with Harold Hunt, published in 1965.

SAMUEL SHEPARD, JR.—*Assistant Superintendent of Elementary Education, St. Louis Public Schools.* Dr. Shepard's past professional experience includes both teaching and administration. He has been an elementary principal and has held several appointments as a supervisor and a director in St. Louis' Central Office. On several occasions Dr. Shepard has been a part-time faculty member at the college level. He has received many awards for his service and leadership to education from distinguished colleges and universities including an "Honorary Doctor of Laws" by the University of Michigan. Dr. Shepard received his Ph.D. in Education from the University of Michigan and has published widely in professional journals. Recently he served as an educational consultant in American Samoa.

CHARLES E. STEWART—*Director of Teacher Education, Detroit Public Schools.* Dr. Stewart has served the profession as a teacher, principal, supervisor, and central office administrator. He has taught summers at Atlanta University, University of Michigan, New York University, and Northwestern University. Dr. Stewart has also taught at Wayne State University where he received his Ed. D. He distinguished himself as director of Human Relations for the Detroit Public Schools prior to assuming his present position. Dr. Stewart has published widely in the area of urban education, race relations, and the teaching of the disadvantaged.

PAUL N. YLVISAKER—*Commissioner, Department of Community Affairs, State of New Jersey.* Dr. Ylvisaker, prior to his appointment as Community Affairs Commissioner, has held many positions concerned with urban and regional problems. He was director of Public Affairs for the Ford Foundation and served as Executive Secretary and later as a consultant to the Mayor of Philadelphia. Dr. Ylvisaker was an Instructor and Tutor in the Department of Government, Harvard University where he received his Ph.D. in Political Economy and Government. He has contributed to the literature with many publications and articles, ranging from *Life* to professional journals. He has been a member of a United Nations planning team in Japan and has served on several Presidential task forces and advisory committees.

EDUCATION AND URBAN SOCIETY

*an independent quarterly journal of
social research with implications
for public policy*

Editor: LOUIS H. MASOTTI, *Department of Political Science, Case
Western Reserve University*

Associate Editors: JAY D. SCRIBNER, *Alfred North Whitehead Fellow,
Graduate School of Education, Harvard University*
R. J. SNOW, *Department of Political Science, University of California at Santa Barbara*

Book Review Editor: MICHAEL DECKER, *Institute of Public Administration, Pennsylvania State University*

POLICY

During recent years an increasing number of social scientists have been conducting research on education as a social institution. Research studies have not been limited to the working of the institution however, but have begun to explore educational institutions and processes as agents of social change. Much of this work, of course, centers on the problems and needs resulting from the national concern with improving the urban environment, but also involves the role of education in a society which is urban.

To foster such research and to provide a multi-disciplinary forum for communication, this quarterly journal was launched in November, 1968: an independent journal of social research with implications for public policy.

SUBSCRIPTIONS

EDUCATION AND URBAN SOCIETY is published quarterly during the months of November, February, May and August. Individual subscriptions are $8 ($9 outside the U.S.A.); Institutional subscriptions are $12 ($14 outside the U.S.A.).

Correspondence concerning advertising, reprints, circulation, and books for review should be addressed to Sage Publications, Inc. at the address below.

SAGE PUBLICATIONS, INC. / 275 So. BEVERLY DR. / BEVERLY HILLS, CAL. 90212

A *Must* Book for all concerned with Urban Education!

EDUCATING AN URBAN POPULATION
Implications for Public Policy

Edited by MARILYN GITTELL, Professor of Political Science, and Director, Institute for Community Studies, Queens College of the City University of New York; Editor, *Urban Affairs Quarterly*.

CONTENTS

INTRODUCTION . . . . . Gittell

I. DEMANDS ON SCHOOL POLICY: THE NATURE OF THE PROBLEM
Campbell and Meranto: *The Metropolitan Education Dilemma: Matching Resources to Needs*
Havighurst: *Chicago's Educational Needs—1966*
Sacks and Ranney: *Suburban Education: A Fiscal Analysis*
Buss: *Law and the Education of the Urban Negro*
Hollander: *Fiscal Independence and Large City School Systems*
Glatt and Roaden: *Demographic Analysis as a Tool for Educational Planning*

II. DECISION-MAKING IN THE URBAN SCHOOL SYSTEMS: CASE STUDIES
Crain and Street: *School Desegregation and School Decision-Making*
Rogers: *Obstacles to School Desegregation in New York City: A Benchmark Case*
Rosenthal: *Pedagogues and Power: A Descriptive Survey*
Gittell: *Decision-Making in the Schools: New York City, A Case Study*
Masotti: *Patterns of White and Nonwhite School Referenda Participation and Support: Cleveland, 1960-1964*

III. SOLUTIONS AND GOALS: ACHIEVING CHANGE
Hirsch: *Planning Education Today for Tomorrow*
Derr: *Urban Educational Problems: Models and Strategies*
Klopf and Bowman: *Preparation of School Personnel to Work in an Urban Setting*
Pettigrew: *Extending Educational Opportunities*
Minar: *The Politics of Education in Large Cities*

INDEX

320 pages, tables, charts, diagrams

Available for immediate shipment!   Clothbound, $7.50 net

SAGE PUBLICATIONS, INC. / 275 South Beverly Drive / Beverly Hills, California 90212

AFFIRMATIVE SCHOOL INTEGRATION

Efforts to Overcome De Facto Segregation in Urban Schools

Edited by Roscoe Hill, *Yale University*, and Malcolm Feeley, *New York University*

With a Foreword by James S. Coleman, *Johns Hopkins University*

A comparative analysis of eight case studies on the legal and political problems complicating the elimination of de facto school segregation in eight northern American cities which were originally prepared as background for *Equality of Educational Opportunity* (the "Coleman Report"). The greater portion of the material compiled for these studies has never been published (not even by the government!).

This volume covers for each of the eight cities (Evanston, Berkeley, New Haven, Pasadena, St. Louis, Albany, San Francisco, and Chicago) the following questions: (1) What specific issues arose in the context of the particular city studied? (2) How did school boards handle the issues? (3) When action was taken by the board, where did the proposal originate and how was it subsequently modified? (4) What role did the courts play? (5) Did the question of the legality and/or morality of distributing school children by race come up? Who raised it? How was it resolved? (6) Did the board succeed in (a) achieving significant statistical change in racial imbalance, and (b) in resolving community conflict over the issue?

The book also contains multi-disciplinary review essays of recent studies on race and education, and a selective bibliography on de facto school segregation. Contributors include: William G. Buss, Jr., William Cohen, James S. Coleman, John E. Coons, Ira Michael Heyman, Harold Horowitz, John Kaplan, Robert Marden, Ralph Reisner, Arnold Rose, Richard D. Schwartz, Michael Usdan, Clement Vose, and Meyer Weinberg.

AFFIRMATIVE SCHOOL INTEGRATION is based upon the November, 1967 issue of the *Law and Society Review,* and is published in cooperation with the Law and Society Association.

January, 1969   160 pp. $6.95   Cloth   L.C. 68-59371

SAGE PUBLICATIONS, INC. / 275 So. Beverly Dr. / Beverly Hills, Cal. 90212

" . . . an attempt to identify the factors that account for resistance to reorganization of school districts in metropolitan areas."

METROPOLITAN AREA SCHOOLS

Resistance to District Reorganization

By BASIL G. ZIMMER, *Professor of Sociology, Brown University,* and AMOS H. HAWLEY, *Professor of Sociology, University of North Carolina (Chapel Hill)*

This volume grew out of an extensive study (funded by the U.S. Office of Education) based on lengthy interviews with hundreds of residents and public officials in six metropolitan areas. The authors analyze use of the schools, knowledge and participation in school related activities, comparative evaluation of city and suburban schools (especially in terms of parents' and officials' satisfaction levels), taxation, views on sources of school support, views on reorganization of school districts, socio-economic and political factors related to resistance to change, and the attitudes of public officials toward schools and changes.

The nature of their findings led the authors to conclude that, in certain types of metropolitan areas, reorganization can be ruled out (because such measures could not be passed in any referendum). And, in those areas where reorganization is a workable alternative, the authors note that totally *different* campaigns for support of such proposals must be conducted in the suburbs (where the major effort must be focused to carry them) and the central city.

METROPOLITAN AREA SCHOOLS is a fascinating and well-documented analysis of the social, economic and political factors which influence crucial policy decisions affecting the education of millions in central cities and their suburbs.

December, 1968   320 pp.   80 Tables   Cloth $7.95

SAGE PUBLICATIONS, INC./275 So. Beverly Dr./Beverly Hills, Cal. 90212